WOOD AND CANVAS HEROES

*Awards of the
Distinguished Flying Cross
and
Other Airmen Stories*

1927 to December 1941

By James W. Patrick

Wood and Canvas Heroes

Awards of the Distinguished Flying Cross
and Other Airmen Stories

1927 to December 1941

Copyright © 2002 by James W. Patrick

James W. Patrick Publishing
1064 Verona Drive
Fullerton, California 92835

ALL RIGHTS RESERVED. EXCEPT FOR USE IN A REVIEW, THE REPRODUCTION OR UTILIZATION OF THIS WORK IN ANY FORM OR BY ANY ELECTRONIC, MECHANICAL, OR OTHER MEANS, NOW KNOWN OR HEREAFTER INVENTED, INCLUDING XEROGRAPHY, PHOTOCOPYING, AND RECORDING, AND IN ANY INFORMATION STORAGE AND RETRIEVAL SYSTEM IS FORBIDDEN WITHOUT THE WRITTEN PERMISSION OF THE PUBLISHER.

ISBN: 0-9719862-0-7

Library of Congress Catalog Card Number: 2002091656

TABLE OF CONTENTS

Foreword   *v*

Introduction   *ix*

Chapter One
   Bursts of Glory   *1*

Chapter Two
   Extended Duration Flight and Nicaragua   *33*

Chapter Three
   Flight Testing and Expeditions   *55*

Chapter Four
   Rescues and Special Flights   *71*

Chapter Five
   Heroism, Noted Civilians and Developments   *89*

Chapter Six
   Mass Flight and Exciting Rescues   *117*

Chapter Seven
   The Prewar Finale   *133*

Appendix I
　　Early Pilots

Appendix II
　　Medal Procurement, Numbering, and Manufacture

Appendix III
　　Other Awards of Some DFC Winners

Appendix IV
　　Known Numbered DFCs, Pre- and Early World War II

Appendix V
　　Index of DFC Awards - War Department

Appendix VI
　　Index of DFC Awards, U.S. Navy, USMC, USCG

Bibliography

Photographic Credits

FOREWORD

Although the title of this book is Wood and Canvas Heroes, it spans the evolution of flight development with passing ties to lighter-than-air and the first heavier-than-air wood and fabric craft through partial and fully metal aircraft just prior to December 1941. The major emphasis in the book, as noted in the subtitle, is the award of the United States Distinguished Flying Cross (DFC) subsequent to 1926, although there are references to other awards, other airmen and other countries. The author has attempted to include additional data on the person awarded, on the circumstances creating the award (citation), on the presentation of the award, and on unique features of each medal. On this basis, there are also exploits in lighter-than-air craft since many early airmen moved in both mediums and were decorated in either.

Also, whenever possible, there are data in the book on the current location of the award. When available, photographs are included of awards and of the winners of them or of their feat. Sadly, much information is lacking, and it is to be hoped that gaps can be filled in by some future work. The author would very much like to be apprised of comments or any information available from any reader. Contact may be made from information on the membership list of The Orders and Medals Society of America (OMSA) or The Orders and Medals Research Society of Great Britain (OMRS). At time of publication, the author was using an email address of *patcolsc@aol.com*, and could also be found in a city directory for Fullerton, California.

I wish to express my thanks to a number of people, mostly from the OMSA, or members of the U.S. Government. In no particular order, I include OMSA members Nick McDowell, Tom Nier, Adam Rohloff, the late Al Gleim, Dick Whitaker, Roger Sullivan, Alan Menke, Shannon Bohanon, and others with nuggets of information or photographs. Many other OMSA members offered help and encouragement, and I wish I could name and personally thank all.

I received an extra measure of assistance from the following government personnel or offices: USN Library and Awards Departments and USMC Museum at the Washington, D.C. Naval Yard; USMC Air-to-Ground Museum Branch at Quantico, Virginia; USMC Museum at Pensacola, Florida; Department of Heraldry at Fort Belvoir, Virginia; U.S. Army Personnel Reserve Center at St. Louis, Missouri (War Department award cards for 80 persons). Award cards, or citation "letters" were received on 20 each USN and USMC pilots from several of the above sources. Great assistance also came from the Department of the Air Force Center for AF History, Boling AFB, Washington, D.C. and the Air Force Historical Research Agency at Maxwell AFB, Alabama. I wish I could list here the names of all the men and women who were especially helpful, but it would be a long list. Management in these organizations should recognize these people for their extra efforts to assist. They will be named on request.

Data were also furnished by the U.S. Department of the Treasury, Washington, D.C.; USAF Museum at Wright-Patterson AFB; Air University at Maxwell AFB, Alabama; U.S. Naval Academy, Annapolis, Maryland, and the Airmen Memorial Museum, Suitland, Maryland.

I received help and data from the Paul Lawrence Library, Wright State University, Ohio; the Minnesota Historical Society in St.

Paul; and from Purdue University, Ohio. The Missouri State Museum in St. Louis, Missouri, was very helpful and gave me a nice welcome as well. The Smithsonian Institution - National Air and Space Museum; the National Archives; and the Library of Congress were especially helpful in securing photographs.

 # *INTRODUCTION*

BACKGROUND

There have been "Airmen" in the United States Army since the Civil War if one considers the Balloon Observers used during that conflict. Professor T.S.C. Lowe, who had developed an observation balloon, became the first man to send signals regarding battlefield actions, which led to a Balloon Signal Service. It was for this reason that the A r Service was initially made a part of the Signal Corps.

These activities led to a lifelong career for Count Ferdinand von Zeppelin of Germany, who was keenly interested in the balloon ascensions he observed, and who made his first balloon ascent in America during the Civil War. Zeppelin developed the rigid, lighter-than-air craft, which bear his name, which later bombed London in World War I, and perhaps culminated in the burning and crash of the Hindenberg at Lakehurst, New Jersey in 1937.

Development Pioneers. The United States military did little in aviation after the Civil War except to provide occasional funding and to observe new developments in the civilian world. Pioneers such as engineer Octave Chanute perfected the early glider (biplane) in the mid 1890's. Major Thomas Baldwin, who made the first parachute jump from a balloon, was a balloonist and parachutist who gave exhibitions around the world. Baldwin built the first "dirigible balloon", sold the first dirigible to the U.S. Army, and managed a flying school which was significant for turning out pilots for The Great War, now called World War I.

In 1903, Dr. Samuel Langley's powered model aircraft flew

across the Potomac River. With funding from the War Department, he built a "man-carrying" model and a houseboat with catapult for launching it. Two unsuccessful launches (probably due to catapult problems) resulted, and it was left to the Wright brothers to succeed in the first heavier-than-air craft manned flight the same month as Langley's second failure, December 1903.

EARLIEST PILOTS

Civilian and Army. After Wilbur and Orville Wright became the first and second heavier-than-air craft pilots, U.S. pilots were Dr. William Christmas (3), Major Baldwin (4), Lieutenant Thomas E. Selfridge (5), and Glenn Curtiss (6). Eleven years after Langley's failure, Curtiss flew Langley's airplane, which had been refurbished with the assistance of the Smithsonian Institute. Using a pontoon takeoff, Curtiss proved that Langley could have been the first man to fly if only his catapult had not failed. Three of the six men named above (the Wright brothers and Glenn Curtiss) were eventually to be awarded the Distinguished Flying Cross as described later in this book.

Lieutenant Selfridge may be considered the first military aviator, and as a passenger in a flight with Orville Wright on September 17, 1908, became the first man killed in an airplane crash when the propeller of the plane they were in struck a wing wire. Selfridge and Lieutenant Frank P. Lahm had been designated to become the first and second pilots of the new "Dirigible Balloon" and were also assigned to monitor the acceptance tests of the new Wright plane built to Army specifications. Lahm rode on the first flight in the added second seat of the plane. Selfridge then took his fatal flight.

After acceptance tests of the Wright plane, three men were

assigned to receive pilot training at College Park, Maryland. Lieutenants Fred E. Humphries and Frank Lahm received their planned three plus hours followed by a solo flight. Lieutenant Benjamin D. Foulois who had participated in the acceptance tests and was anxious to take the training was sent to College Park. After a few minutes of training, the plane was badly damaged. Foulois was ordered to take the plane to Fort Sam Houston where he proceeded to teach himself to fly in 1910. Foulois served in France in World War I as Brigadier General and Chief of the Air Service, A.E.F. He was later in command of the U.S. Air Service/Army Air Corps, succeeding the first Commander, General Mason Patrick. Patrick, as Major General, had previously superseded Foulois as Chief of Air Service, A.E.F. in May 1918 in France.

Army Air Service. Figure 1, taken in 1912, shows Lieutenant Benjamin D. Foulois as the only pilot, with five enlisted men and a single Wright plane at San Antonio, Texas. Foulois was a strong advocate of aviation, continually pushing for procurement of a new airplane. The story is that his superior officer finally snapped, "Let him have an airplane and break his neck." In 1931 Foulois was the winner of the Mackay Trophy. The Air Service had, of course, grown by many pilots during The Great War starting primarily with the Lafayette Escadrille.

First Naval Aviators. The first naval aviator known to have flown was Lieutenant George C. Sweet who was a passenger of Lieutenant Lahm in 1909 at College Park. In 1910 a civilian, Eugene Ely, later a DFC winner (Chapter Five) took a plane off from a ship at Hampton Roads, Virginia. The same year, 1910, Glenn Curtiss, another civilian and a DFC winner (Chapter Five), who was constructing aircraft, offered to provide training for one U.S. Naval Officer. Lieutenant Theodore G. Ellyson was ordered to North Island, San Diego, California on December 23, 1910 where he became Naval Aviator number 1.

Figure 1: Nucleus of U.S. Army Air Service, 1912. Lieutenant Benjamin Foulois with five enlisted men and a Wright aircraft. Foulois is second from right.
National Air and Space Museum

A photograph taken at Pensacola Naval Station in 1912 shows thirteen men identified as the "First Class of Flying Lieutenants," Figure 2. Four of these men are not listed as having been assigned a naval aviator number, perhaps indicating that they did not succeed. Since the lowest numbered aviator in the class is 15, it would seem that fourteen pilots were trained prior to the "first" class.

Naval Aviators number 1, Theodore G. Ellyson (Curtiss' first seaplane pupil) and number 3, John H. Towers teamed in 1911 in a record overwater flight. Towers, a Vice Admiral, was Naval Air Force's Pacific Fleet Commander, 1942 to 1944. Number 2, John Rodgers, was the first pilot to cross from California to near Honolulu. All became noted pilots or high ranking officers. Commander Rodgers, number 2, was killed in a crash on the Delaware River August 27, 1926. First Lieutenant Alfred A. Cunningham, number 5, was the first U.S. Marine Corps aviator.

Figure 2: An early class of Naval Aviators, 1912, at Pensacola. Left to right, (standing) (number is Naval Aviator ref., Appendix I): H.W. Schofield (28), Beeching, W.M. Corry (23), T.P. Norfleet; (seated, rear) E.C. Haas, E.W. Spencer Jr., R.R. Paunek (27); (seated, front) W.D. Capehart (19), C.K. Bronson (15), W.A. Edwards, A.C. Read (24), E.F. Johnson (25) and G.D. Murray (22). Ecwards was ater a Medal of Honor winner and Commander of Legion of Honor for his rescue of 400 from a burning ship in 1917 as a destoryer commander. Paunek received the DFC (Chapter One). Read commanded the NC-4 in his flight across the Atlantic in 1919.
Pensacola Naval Air Station

However, of the first 28 pilots assigned a Naval Aviator number ending with Harold W. Schofield, only two ever received the Distinguished Flying Cross - Robert R. Paunack and USMC pilot Francis T. Evans - as described later. The first of the numbered Naval Aviators to be killed was number 9, Ensign William D. Billingsley who was thrown from his plane over Annapolis in June 1913 while Lieutenant Towers crashed into the water with the plane but survived with severe injuries.

A Naval Officer, Captain W.I.Chambers was awarded the Medal of the Aeronautical Society in 1912 for "his unusual achievements in being the first to demonstrate the usefulness of the aeroplane in navies..." The author did not find any reference to his having been a pilot. Lieutenant Richard C. Saufley, number 14, set altitude records above 16,000 feet in March 1916, but crashed to his death after 8 hours of an endurance flight in June. In 1916 Third Lieutenant Elmer F. Stone, number 38, was the first U.S. Coast Guard officer assigned to flight training when he was sent to Pensacola.

Appendix I lists names of 27 of the early signal corps Badge Qualified pilots and of 271 men assigned Naval Aviator numbers beginning with number 1.

EARLIEST ACHIEVEMENTS

Aircraft Evolution. Prior to the Great War, aircraft were being developed primarily to ensure that they could take to the air, and stay there for any appreciable time. One of the major improvements, by Glenn Curtiss, was to change from a pusher engine to a forward-mounted engine. The war changed the emphasis into fighting skills, not any general improvement. In the post-war period, there was more emphasis on design and development improvements. The military, having little combat employment for the aircraft, sought new designs that enabled them to set new records.Then with new records to achieve they sought improved designs. It was a push-pull effort. In addition, there were expansions, such as branching into seaplanes, and carrier-based planes, and an enlargement of the pilot population. Eventually, there was change again to improve the fighting capabilities for WWII. These are the influences in the nearly 20 years covered by this book.

Crossing the Atlantic. After the Great War, numerous cash awards were offered for crossing the Atlantic Ocean. The U.S. Navy NC-4, one of three planes making the attempt, succeeded (in two steps) in May 1919. Other flights were unsuccessful until the British pilot/navigator pair, Arthur Brown and John Alcock, crossed from Newfoundland to Ireland. But much was left to come, including the New York-to-Paris challenge, which is near the starting point of this book.

First Flight Around the World. In March 1924, four Douglas-built "World Cruisers," with two airmen each, took off from Santa Monica, California for Seattle, Washington to prepare for the first flight around the world. The aircraft, named *Boston*, *Chicago*, *Seattle*, and *New Orleans* were stalled there by problems until September, but eventually two of the four aircraft made the 26,000-mile trip having touched down in 20 countries, survived five forced landings, and burned out 17 engines. The flight returned to Clover Field, Santa Monica, strewn with rose petals and a throng of 100,000 people. The *New Orleans* may be seen there today at the Museum of Flying, the old Douglas plant site at Santa Monica Airport. Two pilots were later awarded the DFC; Lieutenants Nelson, (Chapter Two) and Lowell Smith (Chapter Three).

AWARDS AND MEDALS FOR AVIATORS

The Collier Trophy was a prestigious award for notable developmental achievements. It was given, among others, to Orville Wright and Glenn Curtiss (twice). The Schneider Trophy was awarded for speed records by seaplanes. It began in 1913 with an award for 45.7 mph and ended in 1931 with a record of 340 mph. James Doolittle was the 1925 winner. The Gordon Bennett Cup was presented in France up to 1920. In the United States the Pulitzer Trophy Prize, offered by the publisher from 1920 to

1925, was won by Bert Acosta (see Chapter One) in 1921. At the U.S. National Air Races in 1930, the Thompson Trophy was offered by the Thompson Company and continued to 1949. Finally, in 1931 the Bendix Trophy races were initiated and also continued to 1949.

A Mackay Trophy was awarded from at least 1912 through the '30's for the "Flight of the Year." The Cheney Award of $500 and a plaque for heroism was presented in the 1930's. There was also a Ligue Internationale Des Aviateurs in Paris, which made annual awards. There was also the Litchfield Trophy, which was given to balloonists in the 1920 - 1930 time period. Many notable pilots won annual custody of these trophies and will be mentioned in later chapters. As to personal medals, during World War I, pilots were eligible for the same military awards as other personnel - the Medal of Honor (MoH) or Distinguished Service Cross (DSC) for heroism, and the Distinguished Service Medal (DSM) for achievement.

A survey of World War I awards indicates at least two army awards of the Medal of Honor to airmen, Frank Luke and Eddie Rickenbacker, who were top aces in the Army Air Service. Some 82 WWI Distinguished Service Crosses were issued to airmen, although at least one of these was for prisoner of war escape. Eddie Rickenbacker alone was awarded 8 DSC's. Three U.S. airmen received the MoH in peacetime: Charles Lindbergh, Richard Byrd, and Floyd Bennett. In 1928, Lieutenant C. F. Schilt, USMC, was awarded the MoH for 10 flights under fire to rescue 18 wounded marines in Nicaragua. Schilt reached the rank of Lieutenant General as Director of Marine Corps Aviation, 1955. In 1926 the U.S. Congress authorized the creation of the Distinguished Flying Cross.

THE DISTINGUISHED FLYING CROSS

When established in July 1926, the Distinguished Flying Cross (DFC) was the third highest U.S. award for heroism or the second highest for extraordinary achievement. The War and Navy Departments coordinated on a design in early 1927. However no award recommendations were made until April 1927.

The Air Corps Act of Congress, Public No. 446, passed by the 69th Congress, July 2, 1926 provided for award of the DFC "to any person who, while serving in any capacity with the Air Corps of the Army of the United States, including the National Guard and the Organized Reserves, or with the United States Navy, since the 6th day of April 1917, has distinguished, or who, after this act, distinguishes himself <u>by heroism or extraordinary achievement while participating in an aerial flight</u>." Underline is by the author. These words were seen in every citation viewed by the author.

A letter of January 22, 1927 from the Secretary of the Treasury to the Secretary of War states that he is instructing the engraver at the mint in Philadelphia to submit designs and models for the two medals approved by the July 1926 Act of Congress (DFC and Soldier's Medal).

<u>**Design.**</u> Various designs were submitted to the Commission for Fine Arts before the Commission approved a design by Arthur E. Dubois and Elizabeth Will. The cover illustrates the obverse of the DFC design, a bronze cross patee on which is superimposed a four-bladed propeller, 1 11/16 inches in width. Five rays extend from the reentrant angles forming a 1-inch square in the center behind the cross. The medal is suspended from its ribbon by a rectangular shaped bar. The ribbon is 1 3/8-inches wide with stripes from the edges of 3/32-inch ultramarine blue, 9/64-inch white, 11/32-inch ultramarine blue, 3/64-inch white,

and a center stripe of 3/32-inch old glory red.

Fabrication. Per a recent letter to the author, the Treasury Department could not locate any specific data as to making of the DFC, other than the letter noted above and the Report of the Director of the Mint for 1927 which non-specifically states: "...20 dies made for Medals, etc." and, "...8,225 bronze medals manufactured at Philadelphia." On February 28, 1929, a War Department letter to the Quarter Master General cancels a prior procurement of 150 DFC medals and authorizes "the purchase of 50 crosses."

Appendix II provides some additional data on the procurement and manufacturing of the medal.

Awards Summary. The awards made from 1927 through most of 1941 fall into five broad groups: U.S. Air Service (Air Corps) - 86, Naval Aviation Personnel - 32, USMC Aviators - 25, U.S. civilians - 10, and foreign nationals - 9. Awards were authorized through General Orders, by Naval Boards, and by Acts of Congress. A number of them were presented directly by the President of the United States. In 1937 a Congressional act authorized the Department of the Treasury to award the DFC to the U.S. Coast Guard, resulting in the first and second awards in 1938. With these two awards included, the total identified names listed in this book is 164 for the period 1927 to December 7, 1941. Five Oak Leaf Clusters were awarded in the period with two more to a prior recipient in 1941 and 1942 (see Chapter Seven). One anomaly included in the book is U.S. Navy award number 33 for an act occurring in 1925 that was not approved until 22 years later (also Chapter Seven).

The majority of awards were for "Extraordinary Achievement" often including courage, but there were awards for "Heroism." All awards can be characterized as acts of men (and one woman) pushing their crude vehicles to the limit - stretching the boundaries of flight for the improvement of science, engineering and the art of flying. Fame, fortune, and a variety of cash awards may have additionally motivated some. A few DFC's during this period were awarded for combat by Marines in Nicaragua, and some for life saving. But the fliers were all contributors to the amazing growth of aviation and provided the steppingstones for WWII airmen and planes and for today's military and commercial aviation and space operations.

Award Sequences and Medal Numbering. The first medals struck were used as "models" for design review by the U.S. War Department and Department of the Navy. The Navy originally had some reservations about the design, but accepted it after the War Department proceeded to make the first awards that undoubtedly included some of these models. The War Department started immediately to number the awards in sequence, and numbered probably most of the early medals, first by engraving and later by securing sequentially impressed medals. Most of these medals are numbered at the base of the cross on the reverse, a few on the rim. Some War Department award records show the medal numbers.

The Navy Department apparently did not number awards and was not interested in numbered medals. However most of the Navy's early medals came from the War Department and were therefore numbered. No data on award or medal numbering have been received from the Navy overall, but only from individual museums or collectors.

Citations. Citations were received on award cards, citation "letters", backs of medals and other sources. Generally in the book, the citations are not quoted verbatim, but rather in excerpts. This was at the discretion of the author, for several reasons. War Department citation data are comprehensively covered in the work noted in the Bibliography by Al Gleim, and would be redundant here. Navy Department citations tend to be presented more fully for Naval and Marine airmen.

CHAPTER ONE
BURSTS OF GLORY
1927

GENERAL

In 1913, Alfred, Lord Northcliffe of England, an early believer in aviation, offered the tremendous prize of £10,000 for a cross-Atlantic flight. Two British pilots started a growing thrust to conquer the Atlantic by flight that peaked in early 1919. By May 1919 a gaggle of British pilots and their planes were gathered in Newfoundland to win the approximately $50,000 prize. Two planes had soon crashed, one on takeoff from the primitive fields, and the other in the ocean, with no lives lost. On June 14th, a third crew, John Alcock and Arthur Brown took off and succeeded in the first non-stop crossing of the Atlantic to Ireland.

In the meantime, three U.S. Navy Curtiss Flying Boats; NC-1, -3, and -4 had lifted off from Newfoundland on May 16, 1919, and had followed a string of 41 Navy Destroyers from Canada to Portugal. Two of the aircraft were forced to land at sea, but the NC-4 flown by Lieutenant Commander Albert Read and Lieutenant Walter Hinton USN with three other crewmen managed to fly to the Azores, to land there May 27, then refuel and continue on to Lisbon, Portugal. All the airmen were feted in the British Isles for their accomplishment. The Navy fliers had not been competing for the prize, and it was awarded to Brown and Alcock. Read was Naval Aviator number 24. Hinton, number 135, later made the first flight from New York to Rio de Janeiro in 1922-23. Hinton later served as pilot in extensive exploration of the tropical jungle. His flights included carrying Captain Albert Stevens who is discussed in Chapters Five and Six. I have seen an award card for Commander Holden G. Richardson, Naval Aviator number 15. He was presented the Navy Cross for the flight of the NC-3 so I suspect that Read and Hinton might have been similarly rewarded.

Raymond Orteig, a New York emigrant from France, presented a $25,000 prize offer in 1919 for a New York to Paris flight. Requiring almost twice the distance as the flight for the Northcliffe prize, it was not considered by anyone for another half dozen years. However, in 1922 James Doolittle took the world distance record from the French by a flight from Florida to San Diego. In 1924, Russell Maughan flew the course from New York to San Francisco beating Doolittle's record and resulting in a DFC award (see Chapter Two). Also in 1924 the U.S. Army Air Corps conducted the first around the world flight, led by Captain Lowell H. Smith. See Chapter Three regarding his award of the DFC.

In 1926 the leading allied WWI pilot, René Fonck of France, a 75-kill ace, teamed up with designer Igor Sikorsky and three other crewmen to take the challenge of the New York to Paris Atlantic crossing. The plane crashed on takeoff and burned, with two of the crew killed.

By 1927, there were more candidates, U.S. and European. Rushing to be first, French pilots Lt. Charles Nungessor, a real life Errol Flynn-type hero, and Francis Coli, both WWI aces, took off from Paris May 7 then disappeared near the North American coast. Lindbergh, rushing to put his plans into motion, left California the next day for New York with his new plane. Clarence Chamberlin, a noted pilot, was waiting in New York to fly the Wright-Bellanca plane which the owner had refused to sell to Lindbergh not believing him competent.

Richard Byrd and his crew crashed in the process of flight testing their tri-motor. By the end of May, all three of these flights were ready, and all three made it across the Atlantic to Paris - but Lindbergh of course was first and won the prize as well as the lasting fame. Three of the six airmen in these three flights won the DFC - Lindbergh, Byrd, and Noville (with Byrd) - see this chapter. In the meantime, America was engaged in such endeavors as the Pan-American flight that initiated DFC awards in the United States.

AWARDS BY THE UNITED STATES WAR DEPARTMENT

The First Ten Awards of the DFC. On December 21, 1926, a group of five aircraft left on a Pan-American goodwill flight. Ten pilots of the United States Army Air Corps manned the aircraft. The flight started at Kelly Field, Texas, proceeded by flying down the West, or Pacific Coast and covered 25 countries in Mexico, Central America, South America and the Caribbean islands. It carried as far south as Valdiva where it started up the east coast from Chile, looped through Cuba, and was completed in Washington, D.C. on May 2, 1927. Commander of the flight, Major Herbert A. Dargue was pilot of the aircraft *New York* with co-pilot 1st Lt. Ennis C. Whitehead. The other aircraft and pilots of the Pan-Am mission are as follows:

Aircraft	Pilot	Co-Pilot
San Antonio	Capt. Arthur B. McDaniel	1st Lt. Charles McK. Robinson
San Francisco	Capt. Ira C. Eaker	1st Lt. Muir S. Fairchild
St. Louis	1st Lt. Leonard D. Weddington	1st Lt. Bernard S. Thompson
Detroit	Capt. Clinton F. Woolsey	1st Lt. John W. Benton

The *Detroit* was destroyed in an accident at Buenos Aires February 26, 1927, killing both Woolsey and Benton. They thus became the first two pilots to be awarded the DFC posthumously. All ten of these men were recommended for the DFC by

General Mason M. Patrick, Chief of Air Corps, on April 27, 1927, and were approved by the Secretary of War on May 2, 1927. Dargue (Figure 3) became the first man awarded the DFC as noted on his award card. On the same date, the President of the

Figure 3: First person awarded the Distinguished Flying Cross, Major Herbert A. Dargue. He is shown as a General wearing his Signal Corps Military Aviation Badge as well as his Command Pilot wings. He was killed in a plane crash just after Pearl Harbor. *National Air and Space Museum*

United States presented DFC Certificates of Award for "EXTRA-ORDINARY ACHIEVEMENT" as seen in Figure 4. Calvin Coolidge had been waiting at Boling Field at Washington, D.C. for the ceremony.

Figure 4: President Coolidge, center, presents Distinguished Flying Cross Certificates to Major Dargue, left, and Captain Eaker, right. The other six living Pan-Am fliers were lined up three on each side in a photo seen by the author, but which could not be located for reproduction. Photograph, May 2, 1927, Washington, D. C. *National Archives and Records Administration*

Certificates for Benton and, perhaps, Woolsey were issued May 7, 1927 to their widows. War Department General Orders (WD GO) No. 6, May 18, 1927, Sections I and II are the authority for these awards. The award cards obtained from the Army Personnel Center for these men are numbered in sequence according to rank and seniority[1] of the surviving pilots, then the two deceased pilots, as follows:

Name	Dates (Awards 05-02-27) Presentation	No. Award	Medal
Maj. Herbert A. Dargue	12-21-27	1	(4)²
Capt. Arthur B. McDaniel	12-21-27	(2)	(5)
Capt. Ira C. Eaker	12-21-27	3	none
1st Lt. Leonard D. Weddington	12-21-27	4	(7)
1st Lt. Bernard S. Thompson	12-21-27	5	(8)
1st Lt. Charles McK. Robinson	12-21-27	6	(9)
1st Lt. Muir S. Fairchild	12-21-27	7	(10)
1st Lt. Ennis C. Whitehead	12-21-27	8	(11)
Capt. Clinton F. Woolsey	06-28-28 (posthumous)	(9)	(12)
1st Lt. John W. Benton	03-10-28 (posthumous)	10	13

It has been reported, to the author from Maxwell Air Force Base that Eaker's medal, in their custody, is not numbered. However, Eaker's medal is engraved in two lines as follows:

CAPTAIN IRA C. EAKER, A.C.
U.S. ARMY

The medal is stamped BB&B BRONZE.

Medal No. 13 for Benton is marked on his award card. Benton was buried at the Presidio in San Francisco, and Woolsey in Michigan.

It would appear that all Pan-Am fliers received Chile's Orden Al Merito (Order of Merit) in grade either "Officer," higher rank, or "Caballero," but award cards were not received to substantiate this.

Unfortunately for their record for posterity, these Pan-Am pilots were not awarded the medal itself on May 2, 1927. The eight living pilots were presented the Cross by the Secretary of War Dwight F. Davis, at the Pan-American Union Building in

Washington, D.C. December 21, 1927 and therefore are not usually recognized as the first to be awarded the DFC. The Assistant Secretary F. Trubee Davison and Gen. Mason Patrick commanding the Air Service attended the ceremony. The Mackay Trophy was also awarded for the flight during the December DFC medal presentation. Aviation buffs and medals collectors have long held the view that Lindbergh was the first man to win the DFC but he was actually the eleventh.

On March 10, 1928 Benton's widow was presented the medal privately in San Francisco per her wishes at her residence (presentation of Woolsey's medal is unknown). The reasons for the time lapse between award of the medal in May and its presentation to the eight living pilots in December are not recorded on any material received by the author. It appears that the most likely reason is that in early May 1927, there were not 8 or 10 medals available to be presented.

Herbert Arthur Dargue graduated from West Point in June 1911, and became a flight Lieutenant in the Air Service (circa 1914). Serving under Captain Foulois, he was part of the first Aero Squadron during the Mexican Punitive Expedition. He was one of a half dozen senior officers in 1925 who provided support to Billy Mitchell during his court-martial, all at the risk of their own careers. For the Pan-American flight, he was also awarded the Orden Al Merito, grade of Officer, by the Chilean government.

In 1937 he was at Maxwell AFB as a Lieutenant Colonel in company with many future WWII leaders (including Major Eaker). In 1941, Major General Dargue was placed in command of the First Air Force at Mitchel Field. His awards include the Mexican Service and WWI Victory, American Defense, and four South American decorations. He died in an air accident in California, December 12, 1941, while enroute to Hawaii to take command of the post Pearl Harbor Air Forces in Hawaii and was awarded the DSM posthumously. His son, Donald, was in the West Point Class of 1943, flew in the 8th AF, was a German POW, and retired in 1966 as Lt. Colonel.

McDaniel entered the Air Service for training in 1921. In 1927, Major Dargue chose him as second in command of the Pan-Am Flight. McDaniel was promoted to Brigadier General in 1942 and placed in charge of the III Reconnaissance Command. His medals, including 4 South American and one Italian order, are located at Kelly AFB in San Antonio, but with a substitute DFC (WWII style) and are shown in Figure 5.

Eaker received the Orden Al Merito, grade of Officer also. He later received the first ever Oak Leaf Cluster to the DFC on April 6, 1929 (Chapter Three). This was for service as relief pilot of the 150-hour endurance and refueling flight of the airplane *Question Mark*, at Los Angeles January 1-7, 1929. He later became Commanding General of the Eighth Air Force in WWII, succeeding General Carl Spaatz. His medals at Maxwell Air Force Base, Alabama, include a DFC that is a Bailey Banks and Biddle manufacture (BB&B Bronze), and is named but unnumbered according to communication to the author from Maxwell AFB. His other awards include the DSM, Legion of Merit, and numerous foreign awards[1].

Fairchild, who had served in the 11th Aero Squadron in France in WWI, was wounded in action (WIA) in 1918, received the French Croix de Guerre with four bronze service stars, Italian War Service Ribbon, and was awarded the Purple Heart for his wound in 1932. The Air University Library at Maxwell AFB is named for General Muir S. Fairchild, first commander of the Air University from 1946 to 1948. Fairchild was born September 2, 1894 in Washington, and died March 17, 1950 at Fort Meyer, Virginia.

Bursts of Glory

Figure 5: Some awards of General Arthur McDaniel. From top left; the DFC, Venezuela Order of the Liberator, and the Order of the Sun of Peru. From bottom left; Bolivia Order of the Condor of the Andes, Chile Order of Merit, and the Order of the Crown of Italy. The DFC is not his original issue.
Photo by Shawn M. Bohannon, San Antonio Air Logistics Command

Fairchild and Lieutenant Oakley G. Kelly planned a transcontinental flight in 1923. Fairchild was forced to withdraw when injured in a crash and Lieutenant John A. MacReady replaced him. MacReady and Kelly were awarded the DFC in 1929 retroactively (see Chapter Two). Major Charles Robinson received the decoration and diploma Chilean Orden Al Merito grade of Caballero. His DFC was last known in the hands of his family.

Major Ennis C. Whitehead received the same Al Merito. Major General Whitehead commanded the Fifth Air Force in Douglas MacArthur's Far East Air Forces (FEAF) under Lieutenant General George C. Kenney in World War II. The Fifth Air Force was the command designated the Assault Air Force for the Philippines invasion. Whitehead later was Deputy commander to Kenney, who also held the position as Air Force Commander for MacArthur's SouthWest Pacific Command in World War II. Whitehead was later a Lieutenant General commanding the U.S. Air Defense Command in 1951.

Charles A. Lindbergh, First Person Decorated. On May 20 and 21, 1927, Charles Lindbergh made his historic New York-to-Paris flight to an overwhelming international acclaim. As a consequence, when Lindbergh was returned to the United States by the U.S. Navy, the public gave him a tumultuous greeting. The federal government responded as approvingly as the general public. The President on June 1, 1927 had directed the award of the DFC to Lindy and it was accomplished by WD GO No. 8, June 4, 1927 Section IV. On June 6, 1927, the Adjutant General's Office (AGO) addressed a letter to the Quartermaster General: "The Secretary of War directs that the Distinguished Flying Cross authorized for Captain Charles A. Lindbergh, Air Corps Reserve, in letter from this office dated May 31, 1927 - be engraved Charles A. Lindbergh on the reverse of the cross, the cost of the engraving to be borne by the War Department."

The number 1 appears on the reverse of the medal at the base of the lowest arm, and is engraved rather than stamped (impressed) as on later medals identified in this article, leading to the view that the medal was a prototype. This may be further borne out by the fact that the BB & B BRONZE marking on the reverse is at the top of the medal, not the bottom as on subsequent medals.

Further evidence is the fact that the New York Times reported that on June 2, 1927 "arrangements have been made to have the first Distinguished Flying Cross ready so that President Coolidge may bestow it on Captain Lindbergh after his arrival in Washington. Captain Lindbergh will be the first actually to receive this medal and will get the first one struck." The same article further supports this. "Citations for the medal were awarded to the Army Pan-American fliers when they returned this spring from their swing around South America, but the medals have not been prepared."

Much of official Washington turned out on June 11 as President Coolidge presented Lindbergh with his DFC - see Figure 6. While no official award card was found, the Missouri Historical Society provided data on the medal. This DFC is currently on display in the Society's Lindbergh exhibit at the Missouri State Museum, St. Louis, MO. Figure 7 shows Lindbergh wearing the medal on the day of its award. The award to Lindbergh was for "EXTRAORDINARY ACHIEVEMENT" and "...his courage, his skill, and his resourcefulness."

Figure 6: President Coolidge bestows the DFC on Lindbergh amidst cheers, June 11, 1927. An enthusiastic crowd surrounded the base of the Washington Monument. Lindbergh's mother is standing behind him to the right.
Missouri Historical Society, St. Louis

Name	Dates		No.	
	Award	Presentation	Award	Medal
Capt. Charles A. Lindbergh	06-01-27	06-11-27	11	1

Bursts of Glory

Figure 7: A just promoted Colonel Charles Lindbergh, wearing his DFC, is standing by his mother. President and Mrs. Coolidge are at left. The photo was taken at the temporary White House, June 11, 1927.
Missouri Historical Society, St. Louis

Figure 8 shows the reverse of Lindbergh's DFC. Lindbergh's Award Certificate is shown in Figure 9.

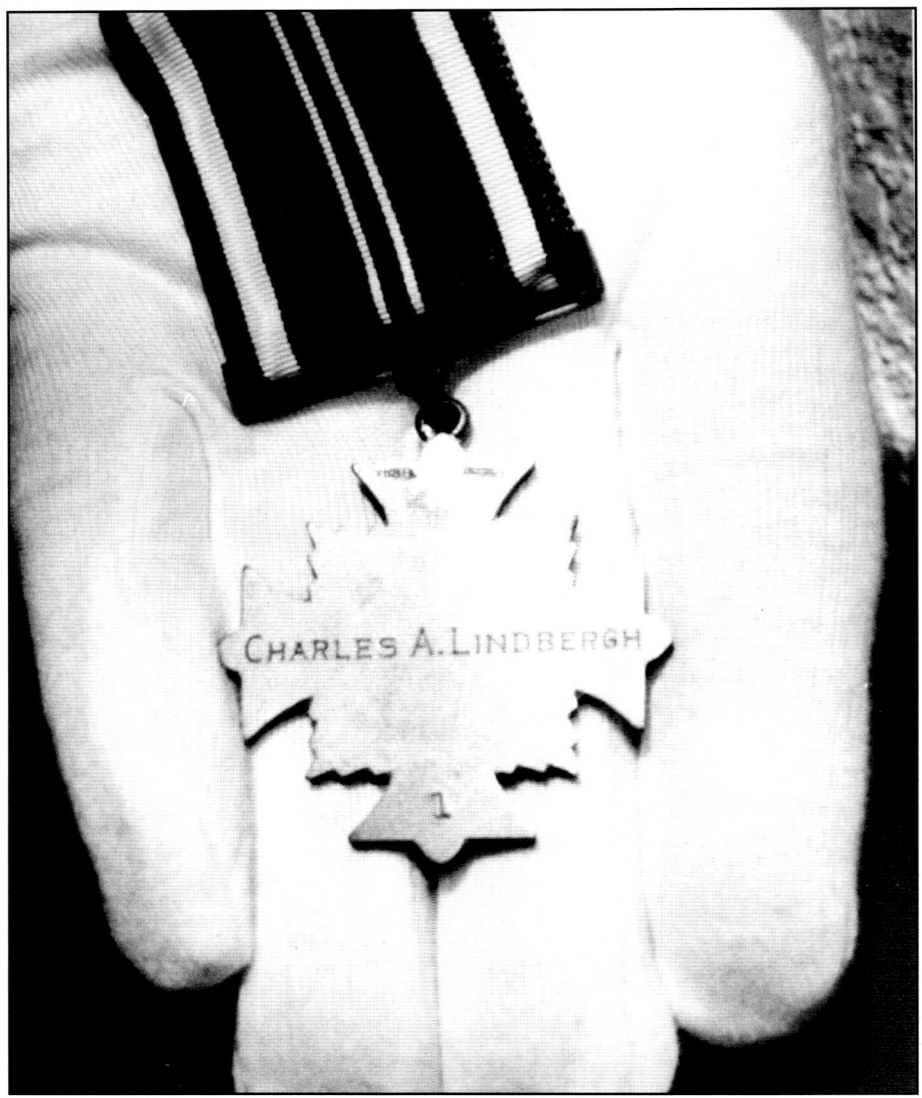

Figure 8: Reverse of Lindbergh's DFC, engraved with number "1" and his name. Note the Bailey Banks and Biddle hallmark on the upper arm.
Photo by J. W. Patrick, Courtesy Missouri Historical Museum

Figure 9: Lindbergh's Award Certificate for the DFC signed by Secretary of War Davis. Original size: 14 3/8 x 12 3/4, according to information received.
St. Louis, Missouri Historical Society

Lindbergh was subsequently awarded the Medal of Honor by Act of Congress. A visit to Lindbergh's grave at a remote and lonely spot near Hana on the Island of Maui, Hawaii speaks of his life as The Lone Eagle and his later isolation. The author noted a pair of U.S. Naval pilot wings left on his headstone by some worshipful if uninformed admirer. The headstone is engraved "...If I take the wings of the morning, and dwell in the uttermost parts of the sea."

To Hawaii, Second and Third Decorations. On June 28-29 1927, pilot Lester Maitland and assistant pilot - navigator Albert

Hegenberger, both Army Air Corps, flew 2,400 miles from Oakland to Honolulu, the longest distance yet traveled over open ocean. The flight was conducted in a tri-motor Fokker-type aircraft. The War Department awarded each a DFC per WD GO No. 16, July 1927 "FOR 'EXTRAORDINARY ACHIEVEMENT', ...in connection with the testing and development of the Air Corps System of Instrument Flying and Landing." The 26-hour flight was largely navigated using radio beacon and sextant.

Hawaii joyously welcomed these airmen and their return to San Francisco was the signal for unbounded enthusiasm according to the New York Times account of the day. The award card for Lt. Hegenberger and other sources for both officers provide the following award data:

Name	Dates		No.	
	Award	Presentation	Award	Medal
1st Lt. Lester J. Maitland	07-14-27	09-29-27	(12)	(2)
1st Lt. Albert F. Hegenberger	07-14-27	09-29-27	13	3

Certificates were presented by the Secretary of State at Boling Field July 21, 1927 with the notation on the award card "crosses not then ready"! The President presented the decorations at the White House September 29, see Figure 10. Note the wearing of swords at this official ceremony, somewhat anachronistic for aircraft pilots. Hegenberger later was awarded the Oak Leaf Cluster (OLC) in 1934 (see Chapter Four). He also was awarded the Decoration and Diploma of Grand Officer of the Order of the Crown of Italy.

Perhaps these two medals were also prototypes as well as Lindbergh's. Subsequent to this presentation, the eight surviving members of the Pan-American fliers were decorated in December as noted above.

Bursts of Glory

Figure 10: President Coolidge presents DFC to Lieutenant Hegenberger as Lieutenant Maitland waits to the left, September 29, 1927. The awards were for their July 27-28 flight to Hawaii in an Army Fokker C-2 Monoplane.
National Air and Space Museum

Hawthorne C. Gray, First Award for Heroism, WD GO No. 5, 1928.
Captain Gray who had been a 2nd Lieutenant in the Idaho National Guard, enlisted as a private in the Army for the Mexican Punitive Expedition. He later was commissioned into the infantry in 1917 but served in Hawaii during the Great War. He then took pilot training, becoming qualified for heavier-than-air craft, balloons, and dirigibles as a pilot in the Army Air Corps.

He participated in U.S. balloon races winning third place in the National race in 1926. This qualified him for participation with the U.S. international team, where he took second place in the 1926 International Gordon-Bennett race out of Belgium making him very well known in the United States.

As an engineering officer at Scott Field, he was aware of various science and engineering questions about flight in the stratosphere. However, he was also undoubtedly motivated to establish a new altitude record and he pioneered a decade of high altitude expeditions. All of his flights, described below, were conducted in open gondolas.

His first attempt, in March 1927, resulted in his passing out at 27,000 feet, while his balloon continued on to 28,500 and then began a rapid descent. When he regained consciousness, he was dropping at 1,200 feet per minute. As he frantically slashed his ballast bags, he slowed the rate sufficiently to survive a hard landing. He had a new U.S. altitude record, but was short of the world balloon record of 35,424 feet, and the airplane record of 40,820 feet. His citation describes his missions as below.

On March 9, 1927, he attempted to establish the world's altitude record, but due to faulty oxygen apparatus he fainted at an altitude of 27,000 feet, recovering consciousness after 52 minutes when his balloon, having overshot its equilibrium point, [28,500 feet], descended to an atmosphere low enough to sustain life.

"Undaunted by this experience, Capt. Gray on May 4, 1927 made a record attempt when he attained an altitude of 42,470 feet, higher than any other earth creature has ever gone. On his descent, however, his balloon failed to parachute and it was necessary for him to descend from 8,000 feet in a parachute [bail out]. With faith still unshaken, and displaying great courage and self-reliance, Capt. Gray on November 4, 1927 made the third attempt, [Figure 11], which resulted in his making the supreme sacrifice. Having attained an altitude of 42,000 feet, he waited for ten minutes, testing his reactions, before making a last rapid climb to his ceiling and a more rapid descent to safe atmosphere. Undoubtedly his courage was greater than his supply of oxygen which gave out at about 37,000 feet. Such high-altitude flights were never again attempted in such an open gondola."

Figure 11: Balloonist Hawthorne C. Gray preparing for his balloon ascension of November 4, 1927. Gray is wearing his heavy gear for the flight to over 40,000 feet in an open gandola.
National Air and Space Museum

Name	Dates		No.	
	Award	Presentation	Award	Medal
Capt. Hawthorne C. Gray	02-18-28	08-29-28	14	20
Presented Posthumously to his widow				

Figure 12 shows Gray's DFC. The medal with ribbon and lapel pin are in a blue leather covered case with pearl clasp release. The lapel pin is marked BB & B and 8 kt. (gold). The DFC with engraved naming and impressed number 20 was intended for presentation to the widow of Captain Gray, but was inadvertently mailed to her direct by registered mail on or about July 10,

1928. As a result, the War Department by mail requested that the Commanding General, Ninth Corps Area "...communicate with Mrs. Gray as ascertain whether she desires a formal presentation of the cross, and if so that the cross be obtained from her and formally presented...."

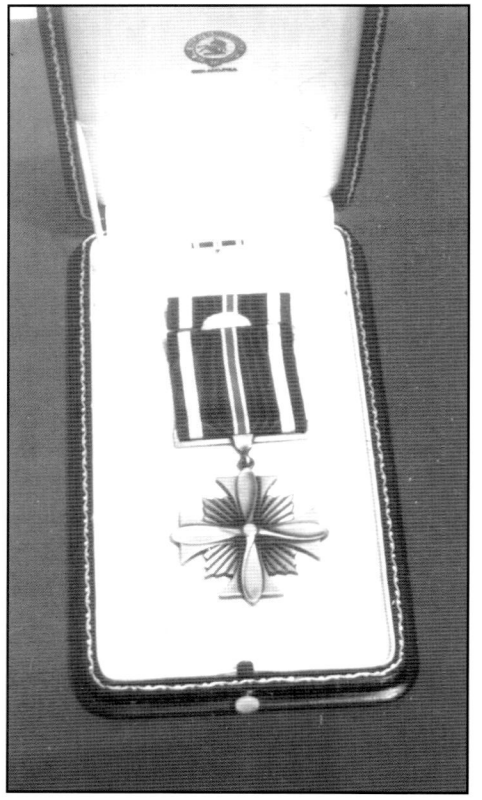 

Figure 12: Gray's DFC obverse in its rare pearl button medal box with ribbon bar and 8kt. gold lapel pin. the medal box contains the logo of Bailey Banks and Biddle on the underside of the lid. The reverse of the medal shows his name, with the impressed number 20 and the BB&B/Bronze hallmark on the base of the lower arm of the cross.
Photo by J. W. Patrick

This was done, and the ceremony of presentation took place at the Presidio of San Francisco, California at 10:45 am Wednesday, August 29, 1928 for the benefit of Mrs. Gray and her two small children. This medal is in the hands of a private collector.

This ceremony completed 1927's fourteen awards by the War Department/Air Service.

AWARDS TO THE UNITED STATES NAVY

General. U.S. Navy pilots twice set world altitude records while flying a class C Seaplane. Lt. C. C. Champion set an altitude record of 37,995 feet with an Apache seaplane. Three weeks later, with the plane converted to landing gear, he set a record for all types of aircraft of 38,419 feet which stood for two years. The aircraft carriers USS *Saratoga* and *Lexington* were commissioned in November and December, respectively. The first Navy DFCs were awarded just over two months after the Army's.

Expedition from N.Y. to France. From June 29 to July 1, 1927, a trans-Atlantic flight was carried out by a four-man crew in the aircraft *America*. The flight was commanded by Lieutenant Commander, later Rear Admiral Richard E. Byrd. The U.S. Navy award card data for Byrd indicates that his award was "authorized by SECNAV Boards 1921 to 1931 {and} approved by Curtis D. Wilbur, Secretary of the Navy." The award read, "...in aerial flight as Commander of the expedition on the airplane *America* that flew from New York to France under extremely arduous conditions, landing safely after 39 hours and 56 minutes..." In fact, the flight reached Paris, but could not land due to visibility and storm conditions, returned to the coast of France and landed in the breakers on the shore at Ver-sur-Mer.

Wood and Canvas Heroes

Byrd's crew included pilots Bert Acosta, Bernt Balchen, both civilians and flight engineer Lieutenant George O. Noville (see Figure13). Two of these men, Byrd and Noville received the first two U.S. Navy awards of the DFC, both of which were presented by the Secretary of the Navy on the same night in New York City, July 19, 1927. This ceremony was held just two days before the awards to Maitland and Hegenberger and two months before they received their medals, and were therefore the second and third actual presentations of the DFC.

Figure 13: The disheveled looking crew of the aircraft *America* just after their crossing from New York to France and landing in the ocean at Ver-sur-Mer. From left; George Noville, Richard Byrd, Bert Acosta and Bernt Balchen; July 1927.
National Archives and Records Administration

The July 20, 1927 New York Times article was headlined "Air Heroes Guests of City at Dinner; Two Get Crosses". The dinner guests included Byrd's four man crew and Clarence Chamberlin who had completed the first non-stop flight from New York to Germany. The column also quoted Secretary Wilbur as stating the Navy lacked authority to award DFCs to Acosta and Balchen because they were non-Naval personnel. On another occasion President Coolidge is quoted in the Times as desiring to award the DFC to Chamberlin, however Chamberlin, a civilian, stated that he would need to join the reserves to qualify, and he declines to do this.

Information to the author is that Byrd's medal is not numbered so Noville's was probably not either. This might indicate that these were also prototype models. Since Byrd was the senior officer, the author assumes that he got the first naval medal and Noville the second[3].

Name	Dates		Medal
	Award	Presented	No.
1. Commander R. E. Byrd	07-13-27	07-19-27	none
2. Lieutenant G. O. Noville	07-13-27	07-19-27	tbd

Byrd's medal was acquired at auction from England in 1988 and is held by a private collector. His medal is engraved in the Navy style in seven lines as follows:

COMMANDING
AIRPLANE
> AMERICA <
COMMANDER R.E. BYRD, U.S.N.
IN
TRANSATLANTIC FLIGHT
JUNE 29-30, 1927

Byrd was a dedicated air explorer who teamed with a number of pilots in his trips. Although qualified as a pilot, Byrd seemed to realize that he served best as navigator. His major expeditions were conducted in Tri-motors with a crew of four.

Byrd was a Lieutenant in 1918 and served as the commander of the U.S. Naval Air Station, Halifax, Nova Scotia. In 1919 Byrd was developing and testing navigational equipment in plans to cross the Atlantic. He first teamed with Floyd Bennett when they had flown 6,000 miles in the MacMillan Arctic expedition in 1925. As Lieutenant Commander, Byrd had commanded the Naval Air Detail.

Byrd and Floyd Bennett made a flight from Spitzbergen, Norway to the North Pole on May 9, 1926 in a Fokker Tri-motor. While full success is latterly in some dispute, Byrd and Bennett were awarded the U.S. Medal of Honor, presented by President Coolidge. Bennett later died of pneumonia after leaving a sick bed to pilot a relief plane attempt in 1928 when von Huenefeld, Fitzmaurice, and Koehl (Chapter Two) had crash-landed in Labrador.

Acosta and Balchen were known as "respected pilots". Acosta was a naval aircraft test pilot, and he had won the Pulitzer Trophy racing prize in 1921 in a Curtiss plane. Balchen was from Norway, and was later the pilot to fly Byrd over the South Pole. Byrd's South Pole expedition climaxed November 28-29,1929. Byrd himself had gone into debt nearly $200,000 to help finance this large expedition. Byrd, with Bernt Balchen, pilot; Harold I. June, U.S. Navy, co-pilot; and U.S. Army Capt. Ashley C. McKinley, USAAF, photographer made the flight in 19 hours in a plane named for Floyd Bennett. For this expedition, Mckinley received a DFC from the War Department (as did others), and June from the Navy as described in later chapters.

1926 Alaska Survey. Lieutenant, later Commander, Ben Harrison Wyatt was the officer commanding an Alaskan Aerial Survey conducted in 1926 and was presented for consideration for a DFC to the BuNav Board April 1927, the first Navy retroactive award. The expedition departed Seattle June 6, 1925, on the tender *USS Ganet*, a barge with photo lab, and three Loening amphibians. The expedition worked on until September on the first aerial mapping of Alaska. A New York Times report datelined Washington Sept. 16, 1927 was headlined "HIGHEST FLYING HONOR WON BY TWO NAVY MEN". The article identified that citations had been issued for Lieutenants Wyatt and Cornwell. " Wyatt's citation is for outstanding achievement in connection with the aerial survey of Alaska in the summer of 1926" it said. "...while Lieutenant Cornwell's is for heroism over Hampton Roads on November 18, 1926."

Wyatt is considered (by the author) the No. 3 Naval award, having been approved August 2, 1927, announced in the New York Times for September 16, and possibly presented mid September. No medal number data have been found. In 1922, Lieutenants Wyatt and George T. Owen flying DH-4Bs, completed a round trip transcontinental flight in short hops. Leaving San Diego, they flew a southern route then up to Washington, D.C., across to San Francisco, and back to San Diego. The flight lasted 15 days and covered 7,000 miles, in about 90 flight hours.

Life Saving Attempt in Aerial Flight -
First USN Heroism Award. On November 18, 1926, Lieutenant (jg) Delbert Strother Cornwell was in flight over Hampton Roads, Virginia. At 2,000 feet, the left wing collapsed, causing a spin. When he called for his passenger Lt. (jg) Edward B. Curtiss to bail out, Curtiss could not free himself from his seat. Despite facing almost certain death, Cornwell attempted to free him, then returned to his seat and attempted to control the plane.

However, the plane crashed to a complete wreck resulting in the death of the passenger and the injury of the pilot. This is USN award No. 4, also approved August 2, 1927 and announced September 16, 1927. The New York Times of September 2, 1929, in an article datelined Pensacola, Fla. September 1, 1929 states: "Two fliers at the naval air station were decorated here yesterday (August 31) with Distinguished Flying Crosses; Lieutenant D.S. Cornwell (who) risked his life, and Lieutenant William Davis who was decorated for his part in the flight across the Pacific..." Rear Admiral A.W. Marshall, commandant of the air station, bestowed the decorations. Davis' award is covered in Chapter Two.

Name	Dates		Medal
	Award	Presented	No.
3. Lieut. B.H. Wyatt	08-02-27	09- ?- 27?	tbd
4. Lieut. jg D.S. Cornwell	08-02-27	08-31-29	tbd

Cornwell was a Captain and Commanding Officer of the carrier *Philippine Sea* in 1946.

"FLYING CROSS AWARDED TO 5 FEDERAL AVIATORS" according to a New York Times article datelined December 14, 1927. These retroactive awards include one Navy pilot as follows and four Marine Corps pilots for flight to Santo Domingo as described later in the chapter.

<u>**Award for Heroism in Dirigible Fire of June 13, 1919.**</u> Lieutenant Commander Robert Rudolph Paunack was recognized in the New York Times article: "[Paunack] at present Executive Officer of the aircraft carrier Langley, received the Cross for heroism in aerial flight on June 3, 1919. The dirigible C-8 while operating at an altitude of 8,500 feet caught fire from a backfiring engine. The commanding officer Paunack seized a

fire extinguisher and climbed out to the nacelle with no handholds nor lifeline and extinguished the fire, saving the ship and crew of six."

Paunack was an early pilot, being Nava Aviator No. 27. His medal is believed to have been presented in 1928. He was later Commanding Officer of NAS San Diego, and retired in 1935 as Commander. Recalled in WWII he served as a staff officer then retired as Captain. He died on September 7, 1979 in Pensacola, age 93, the oldest Naval Aviator. It is interesting that this Navy heroism action, (second heroism award), as well as the first Army award for heroism was for a lighter-than-air aircraft.

Name	Dates		Medal
	Award	Presented	No.
5. Lt. Commander R. R. Paunack	12-13-27	1927/28 ?	tbd

AWARDS TO THE UNITED STATES MARINE CORPS

General. The United States Navy was the authorizing agency for the Marine Corps, and the data show that Marine Corps medals were issued from the same stock as the Naval personnel. As was the case for Naval personnel, the USMC medal award sequence numbers were not recorded on any documents yet seen by the author. One medal number was shown on a Citation letter. The sequence of awards is selected by known dates from other sources by the author as indicated by the number to the left of each individual's name. The first two actions occurred the same date, and perhaps one preceded the other by a short period of time, but the Citation for the first award, Rowell, is dated November 22, 1927, while that of Boyden is dated December 21, 1927. Due to lack of information to the author on dates of approval and presentation, errors may exist.

Heroism in Nicaragua. What is believed to be the first Marine Corps DFC award was for heroism in Nicaragua. Major Ross E. Rowell was cited for Extraordinary "HEROISM" July 16, 1927, "...during an Insurrection in Nicaragua having been notified by his patrol that the garrison at Ocotal, one hundred miles away, was in danger, he at once took to the air, and leading a flight of five planes in the face of a tropical storm, conducted the attack with the highest tactical skill, destroying a greater part of the enemy, thereby saving the little garrison from almost certain destruction."

Rowell led the attack with five DH Aircraft in a strafing and dive-bombing attack against bandit forces at Ocotol, Nicaragua. Diving attacks had been used in The Great War (WWI) and in Haiti, but these were the first conducted according to training doctrine, and "...is considered the first organized dive-bombing attack," according to U.S. Navy documents. Rowell also received the Distinguished Service Medal for service during his 1927-28 activities against the Nicaraguan Bandits.

Rowell had risen from Lieutenant in 1906, and was a student naval aviator in 1923. He received many peacetime awards in gunnery, National Air Races, and efficiency. He was promoted from Brigadier General to Major General and commanded the Marine Aircraft Wings Pacific from Guadalcanal through 1944.

His awards include those mentioned plus the Legion of Merit and many others. His DFC, manufactured by August C. Frank, was probably approved in November 1927, and was presented in 1928 as shown in Figure 14. His award ceremony was held at NAS San Diego, California, with Captain McCrary, USN to Rowell and to Chief Gunners mate Wodarczyk. The medal is engraved:

Major Ross E. Rowell, USMC, Extraordinary Heroism in Aerial Flight 16 July, 1927, During an Insurrection in Nicaragua

Figure 14: Foreground, Captain McCrary waits to present DFCs as Commander Spencer, to his right, reads citations. Major Rowell, left, and Chief Marine Gunner Wodarzyk wait to receive them at Naval Air Station, San Diego.
National Archives and Records Administration

First Lieutenant Hayne D. Boyden, USMC serial number 099, was cited "For having distinguished himself by display of Extraordinary Heroism, initiative, coolness, and excellent judgment when on July 16, 1927, while in command of an air patrol of two planes, he discovered the small Marine Detachment at Ocotal to be besieged by a vastly superior force. Boyden dispatched one plane for reinforcements and then in the face of hostile fire, heroically proceeded single-handed to the attack of the bandit force that had outnumbered the Marine and native garrison."

Starting as a Gunnery Sergeant Pilot, he was commissioned in 1919. In WWII he served in the Pacific Theater as Chief of Staff, 2nd Marine Aircraft Wing. He was promoted to Brigadier General in 1949 on retirement. His awards include the Legion of Merit. He died August 23, 1978 (Asheville, North Carolina?).

Name	Dates		Medal
	Award	Presentation	No.
1. Maj. Ross E. Rowell	11-02-27	09-07-28	63
2. 1st Lt. Hayne D. Boyden	12-21-27	tbd	tbd

Major Rowell's DFC is held at the Museums Branch Hq. U.S. Marine Corps, Quantico, Virginia.

Flight from Washington, D.C. to Santo Domingo, April 1921.
Distinguished Flying Cross awards for four Marines were announced on the same date as the award to Lt. Commander Paunack U.S. Navy, i.e. December 14, 1927. The citation letters were dated December 13. Their flight on April 22, 1921 (23rd according to one citation) was described as the longest unguarded flight of land planes over land and water. Lieutenant Colonel Thomas Turner was commanding officer of the flight. Turner was cited for "Extraordinary Achievement in aerial flight as the commanding officer of the pioneer flight of airplanes to make a flight from Washington to Santo Domingo City, Dominican Republic." His citation letter was addressed to him in Third Brigade, China. He had been commissioned in the USMC in 1902, became a Major and Junior Military Naval Aviator in 1917. He was later detailed to the Army Signal Corps (Aviation). Returning to the USMC in 1918 he was appointed a Naval Aviator and Lieutenant Colonel assigned for service in Haiti. He was twice awarded the Haitian Military Medal for valor, and was two times Chief of Marine Corps Aviation.

First Lieutenant Lawson Sanderson was engineering officer for the flight. His service included Haiti in 1919 and 1922 and in Nicaragua in 1928. He was eventually a Brigadier General in WWII on Guadalcanal serving as Commanding Officer of Marine Air Group 11 on New Hebrides, and commanding the 4th Marine Wing in the Marshalls-Gilberts. Sanderson was later Commanding General of the Marine First Air Wing at Tientsen, China. His awards include the Legion of Merit and many others. His citation was addressed to him at Quantico. He was presented his DFC in Nicaragua. He died June 11, 1979.

Lieutenant Basil Bradley, who had retired at that rank before his award, had the early USMC serial number 100. He was cited "For extraordinary achievement in aerial flight as Executive Officer...." The citation, dated December 13, 1927 was addressed to him at Fitzsimmons General Hospital, Denver, Colorado.

Gunnery Sergeant Charles Rucker was cited as "...mechanic in charge of upkeep of planes and engines...." The citation addressed to him was to Mr. Charles Rucker in West Virginia.

Name	Dates		Medal
	Award	Presentation	No.
3. Lt. Colonel Thomas C. Turner	12-13-27	08-16-29	48
4. 1st Lt. Lawson H.M. Sanderson	12-13-27	08-31-29	62
5. 1st Lt. Basil G. Bradley	12-13-27	tbd	tbd
6. Gunnery Sgt. Charles W. Rucker	12-13-27	tbd	tbd

The year 1927 thus included fourteen War Department, five U.S. Navy and six U.S. Marine Corps awards of which perhaps four to seven were presented the same year.

[1] See Appendix III which also lists other awards or biographical data of DFC winners.

[2] The numbers in parenthesis are not verifiable by the author, and do not appear on the award cards (if any). However the research supports this choice of number for award and medal, if in fact medals were always numbered.

[3] Since no award data from the Navy, including Marine Corps, were found, the author has assigned numbers to the left of each name, based on date information found in research. Medals numbers were not noted in USN data either. The first two awards for Byrd and Noville are clear but some of the sequence is arbitrary.

CHAPTER TWO
EXTENDED DURATION FLIGHT AND NICARAGUA 1928

GENERAL

After the flurry of trans-Atlantic flights, pilots turned in other directions in 1928. Commander Richard Byrd's team made Antarctic history for two years. Two Australians and two Americans formed a crew to fly from San Francisco to Brisbane, Australia. Howard Hughes made his renowned movie "Hells Angels." The first takeoff and landing on the *USS Lexington* (CV-2) was made by a Navy pilot, Lieutenant A.M. Pride.

A noted pilot and the first Naval Aviator, Commander Theodore G. Ellyson and two other pilots, Lieutenant Commander Hugh Schmidt and Lieutenant Roger Ramscheusen were killed in the crash of a Loening Aircraft in Chesapeake Bay on a night flight on February 27 from Norfolk, Virginia to Annapolis, Maryland. A marine pilot, Lt. C.F. Schilt, was awarded the Medal of Honor for rescuing 18 wounded, with ten landings under fire in Nicaragua. Schilt had previously been second in the Schneider Cup Race in 1926 - the last Navy participation. In May 1928, Navy pilots, Lieutenants Arthur Gavin and Zeus Soucek, set a 36-hour duration flight record. Soucek and Lieutenant Lisle Maxson also set Class C seaplane records for load, speed, distance, and duration in the same month.

Amelia Earhart, with an accompanying pilot and mechanic, became the first woman to cross the Atlantic in an airplane. Contracts were released in 1928 for the giant airships *USS*

Akron and *Macon*, and the German airship *Graf Zeppelin* made an around-the-world voyage. Another lighter-than-air aircraft, the semi-rigid dirigible *Italia* crashed after a North Pole flight, killing one and injuring its commander, General Umberto Nobile, on the ground then, with six remaining crew on board, the airship bounded back into the atmosphere and disappeared. Seven nations and 24 planes attempted rescue. The noted explorer Roald Amundsen and five companions in one rescue plane were killed. Another casualty, the expedition scientist Dr. Finn Malmgren, was lost on the ice before rescue succeeded.

AWARDS BY THE UNITED STATES WAR DEPARTMENT

Awards for Distance Flights. The next four awards, made to Lieutenants Goebel, Kelly, MacReady, and Maughan were linked by War Department General Orders No. 4, March 31, 1928, which actually preceded Hawthorne Gray's WD GO of April 14. All awards were for "EXTRAORDINARY ACHIEVEMENT." The four awards were approved February 18, 1928. The New York Times of February 21, 1928, announced "Army Cross awarded for five," combining Gray with the four.

Dole Hawaii Race 1927. In 1927 the Dole Pineapple Company sponsored a competitive prize race to Hawaii. The winner, Lieutenant (later Colonel) Goebel, Air Corps Reserve, made the flight to Hawaii from the U.S. mainland August 16-17, 1927. He was cited for piloting an airplane on a nonstop flight from Oakland, California to Wheeler Field, Honolulu, a distance of 2,400 miles in 26 hours and 17 minutes. He was accompanied by Lieutenant Commander William V. Davis, USN, who later received a DFC from the Navy, see below.

Eight planes started the trip to compete for the prize, but four either crashed trying to take off, or turned back. Two planes were lost enroute, costing the lives of four men and one woman. Two other pilots died in searching for them, and, to take the death toll to ten, three pilots had been killed in preliminary flights. The second place plane, piloted by Paul Schluter and Martin Jensen arrived in Hawaii after 28 hours, 16 minutes. After Maitland and Hegenberger (Chapter One) had flown to Hawaii in June 1927, Emory Bronte (Chapter Five) and Lowell Smith, (Chapter Three) had crossed the Pacific in July 1927. They were then followed by the four Dole finshers just named, in August 1927.

Lieutenant Goebel's DFC certificate was mailed April 11, 1929. Medal presentation to him was August 17, 1928 at the Pacific Southwest Exposition, Long Beach, California by the Commanding Officer, Los Angeles Harbor Defenses. Colonel Goebel was awarded a special medal from the Ligue International des Aviateurs, Paris, in 1929 In addition some six other American pilots based on assistance, from Captain Lester L. Maitland, were given the Ligue Medal.

New York to Coronado Flight, 1923. Lieutenants Kelly and (now) Captain MacReady, both Army Air Service, flew the first trans-continental nonstop flight from Mitchel Field, New York to Rockwell Field, Coronado, California in 10 minutes less than 27 hours, May 2-3, 1923. According to a New York Times news account, "They lunched one day on the Atlantic coast and the next day by the shore of the Pacific." In attempting this flight they failed twice, but set an official record for endurance of 35 hours, 18 minutes, and 30 seconds on one flight.

MacReady was at one time holder of the world's altitude record for a flight to 40,800 feet (37,800 true above sea level) with a single engine LePere biplane. Kelly and MacReady were presented their crosses on July 28, 1928, thus being the first War Department retroactive awardees. MacReady died September

16, 1970 and is buried in Mariposa, California.

New York to San Francisco, 1924. Lieutenant Maughan, Air Service, was cited for a dawn-to-dusk flight in a pursuit plane departing Mitchel Field, NY at 2:58 am June 23, 1924 and landing at Crissy Field, San Francisco, California at 9:47 pm (local times). His trip covered 2,540 miles in 21 hours, 48.5 minutes. His route carried him from New York via Dayton, St. Joseph and Cheyenne to San Francisco. His decoration was presented August 6, 1928 at Fort Douglas, Utah. His DFC was manufactured and marked by BB & B and named in the same style as was Hawthorne Gray's. Maughan was presented an engraved gold medal by the city of San Francisco, made by Shreve & Co., in commemoration of his flight as seen in Figure 15. His medals were acquired by a collector in California in recent years.

Maughan had previously won the Distinguished Service Cross (No. 1954) for combat with the 139th Aero Squadron in WWI, shooting down 4 German aircraft. In 1924 Maughan also took the world's speed record from the French at 236.4 mph. The French had previously taken the record from General Billy Mitchell.

Name	Dates		No.	
	Award	Presentation	Award	Medal
2nd Lt. Arthur C. Goebel	02-18-28	08-17-28	15	(21)[1]
1st Lt. Oakley G. Kelly	02-18-28	tbd	(16)	(17)
1st Lt. John A. MacReady	02-18-28	07-28-28	17	(18)
1st Lt. Russell L. Maughan	02-18-28	08-06-28	18	19

Awards to Foreigners - by Act of Congress. Public No. 342 - 70th Congress, May 2, 1928. On October 8, 1928 WD GO No. 14 awarded 14 DFCs, six of these being to pilots of foreign governments, confirming the prior Act of Congress, plus seven Alaska awards, and another for Heroism.

Extended Duration Flight and Nicaragua

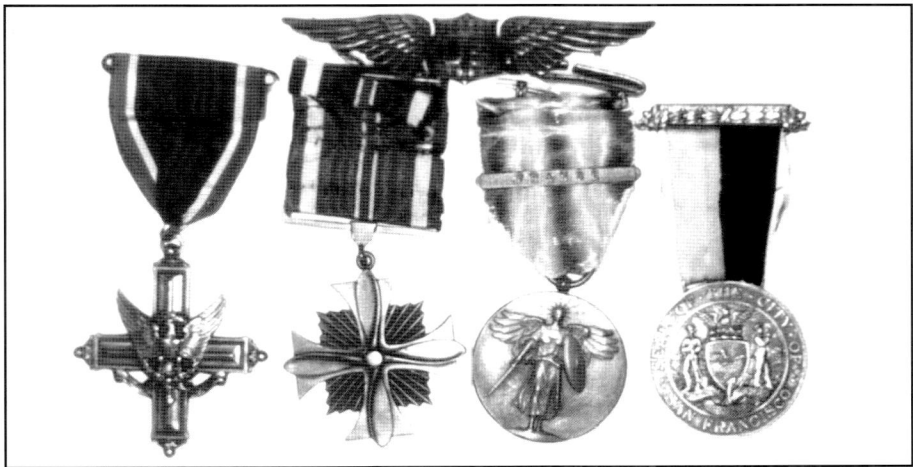

Figure 15: Medals of Russell Maughan include the Distinguished Service Cross (WWI), the DFC, World War Victory Medal and Specia Gold medal from the City of San Francisco, all seen in obverse, below. Above, the reverse of his DFC, number 19, marked as was Hawthorne Gray's. The reverse of the Gold Medal is shown with its inscription: "Lt. Russell I. Maughan, from the People of San Francisco, Commemorating His "Dawn-to-Dusk" flight, from New York to San Francisco, June 23, 1924."
Photo by J.W. Patrick, Courtesy of a Private Collector.

West Across the Atlantic, 1928. The first ever civilian and first foreigner decorated with the DFC was Baron von Huenefeld of Germany who made the first westward nonstop trans-Atlantic flight by airplane from Europe to North America. With his two companions; Major Fitzmaurice, Chief of Irish Free State Air Force, and Captain Koehl, German Air Force, retired, von Huenefeld traveled on March 12 through 13, 1928. The flight was in a metal skin Junkers monoplane, the *Bremen*, and took 36 hours from Dublin to Labrador, where their plane foundered. The pilots were totally lost and out of fuel when they spotted a lighthouse and crash-landed on the northern tip of Labrador. This triggered a rescue effort that cost the life of Floyd Bennett as previously mentioned. The three pilots are shown in Figure 16.

Interestingly, on the award cards for von Huenefeld and Koehl there are notations that state, "Birthplace and residence: apparently Germany?" and for Fitzmaurice - "apparently Ireland" when it also states: "Major, Chief of Irish Free State Air Force". These awards were for "EXTRAORDINARY ACHIEVEMENT" and "...exceptional skill and resourcefulness in making the first westward nonstop flight by airplane from Europe to North America" as stated in the citation. President Coolidge made the presentation of the certificates and medals May 2, 1928 at the White House.

Koehl had received the Prussian Pour le Merite (Blue Max) as a bomber pilot in WWI, and numerous other decorations as listed in *Appendix III*.

An Odyssey Across the South Atlantic. A Colonel in the Italian Air Force (Regia Aeronautica), Marchesi Francesco de Pinedo was recognized for his extraordinary achievement in making an aerial journey of twenty-five thousand miles by flying boat in the course of which he arrived in the United States by air

Extended Duration Flight and Nicaragua

Figure 16: Westward trans-Atlantic flight celebrated by the three pilots, from left; Baron von Huenefeld, and Captain Koehl of Germany, and Major Fitzmaurice of Ireland. The three men flew from Ireland to New York, March 12-13, 1928.
San Diego Aerospace Museum

from Rome. In March 1927, his flight took him from Rome to Africa across the Atlantic, across Brazil, around South America through the West Indies, to New Orleans. Then next to Arizona, back to New York, then Newfoundland, to London to Rome. In total, he flew an amazing four-month, four-continent flight. He was greeted by Mussolini upon his return, and was presented his DFC by the U.S. Ambassador to Italy at the Ambassador's house, October 12, 1928.

South Atlantic Crossing Again. Two French pilots, Lieutenant Dieudonne Costes, French Air Force, and Lieutenant Commander Joseph LeBrix, French Navy, were awarded the DFC for EXTRAORDINARY ACHIEVEMENT for "an extremely hazardous journey of 35,000 miles, in the course of which they arrived in the United States in February, 1928, by air, after making the first nonstop flight across the South Atlantic." This later phrase is quoted from the award card which raises a question in light of de Pinedo's 1927 crossing. The remarkable journey of these two, traveling from October 14, 1927 to April 14, 1928 was from Paris to St. Louis, Senegal, Africa, thence to Port Natal, Brazil, South America, to the United States. They continued across the continent, took a steamer to Tokyo with their plane, and continued their flight across Asia to Paris. Figure 17 shows the decoration which was presented to Costes by the United States Ambassador Herrick, in Paris, on August 29, 1929 just before the ambassador departed for the United States. The two men are shown with their aircraft while traveling through the Panama Canal Zone enroute to the United States in Figure 18.

Figure 17A: Costes' medals, including the reverse of his DFC, number 34, with equivalent markings to Gray's.
Photo courtesy of a private collector

Extended Duration Flight and Nicaragua

Figure 17B: Shown in both obverse and reverse is the Japanese Naval Society Medal to Costes.
Photo courtesy of a private collector

Figure 17C: Special medals presented by Philadelphia and Indianapolis. The latter is inscribed "Presented by the Citizens Of Indianapolis in Recognition of the First Paris-New York Airflight, September 1-8, 1930." "TO DIEUDONNE COSTE" (sic) is inscribed around the upper edge.
Photo courtesy of a private collector

Wood and Canvas Heroes

Figure 18: French pilots with their plane, at France Field, Panama Canal Zone. From left; Lt. Costes, Miss Marjorie Stinson, Lt. LeBrix, and Lt. Col. Fisher. This stop was made while the two lieutenants were enroute from Paris to New York, after crossing the South Atlantic.
National Archives and Records Administration

LeBrix, who had not been present with Costes when the Ambassador presented his DFC, was presented with his medal at the U.S. Embassy in Paris September 28, 1929 when the U.S. Military Attaché, Brigadier Harts, pinned it on in the absence of the U.S. Ambassador. This ceremony is shown in Figure 19.

Costes was irrepressible, flying from Paris to New York in September 1930 with Maurice Bellonte for the first such east-west flight. The two were lionized in New York. They then flew to Dallas, winning a prize of $25,000, then back to Washington, D.C. They were guests of President Hoover at the White House then barnstormed the country. Costes later set a new world distance record of 5,000 miles flying from Paris to Manchuria in 1930.

Extended Duration Flight and Nicaragua

Names	Dates		No.	
	Award	Presentation	Award	Medal
Baron E. Gunther von Huenefeld	05-02-28	05-02-28	19	(14)[1]
Maj. James C. Fitzmaurice	05-02-28	05-02-28	20	(15)
Capt. Hermann Koehl	05-02-28	05-02-28	21	(16)
Col. Francesco de Pinedo	05-02-28	10-12-28	22	(22)
Lt. Dieudonne Costes	05-02-28	03-29-29	(23)	24
Lt.Cdr. Joseph LeBrix	05-02-28	09-28-28	24	(23)

Costes became a pilot in September 19˙2, then served in the Great War. He reached the rank of Lieutenant and was awarded a Croix de Guerre plus 11 citations. He had engaged in 54 combats and 27 night bombardments. He died in 1973. Costes, as might be imagined, had received a variety of awards from a number of countries including the rare gold Imperial Naval Pilot's Society award of Japan. His medals and considerable ephemera were auctioned in Paris, France in 1992. His DFC et al are in the hands of a private co lector.

Figure 19: Brigadier General Harts, American Military attaché in Paris, presents DFC to Lt. LeBrix, September 28, 1928.
Library of Congress

Alaskan Flying Expedition, Summer 1920. In August 1928, the Army recognized the exploits of five officers and 2 enlisted men with the award of the DFC for the mapping of Alaska under the command of 1st Lieutenant/Captain St. Clair Street, Air Service. The pilots are shown in Figure 20. These awards were included in the War Department (WD) General Orders Number 14 of 1928 (GO No. 14, 1928) which also included six foreign nationals previously discussed. Street had previously been awarded the Purple Heart as replacement for his 1919 Meritorious Services Citation Certificate (MSCC) from World War I. He served in the Third Aviation Instruction Center in the American Expeditionary Forces. Awards to these men were announced in the New York Times, datelined Washington August 28, 1928.

Figure 20: Pilots of the Army Alaska air-mapping expedition, 1920. Left to right are Captain St. Clair Street, 1st Lt. C. C. Nutt, and 2nd Lieutenants R. C. Kirkpatrick, E. H Nelson, and C. E. Crumrine.
National Archives and Records Administration

Ross Kirkpatrick had been in the Air Service but was a civilian at time of death, and his award was posthumous. He was survived by his mother in Catalina Island, California, and a wife in Washington. His medal was sent to the Commanding General, 9th Corps Area for presentation. His widow formally received the cross in Los Angeles from Colonel George Hamilton, Cavalry.

Lieutenant Nutt served as pilot and deputy flight commander. He received his decoration at Brooks Field, Texas. First Lieutenant Crumrine was presented his DFC by Major General Edwin B. Winens, Hawaiian Division Commander, at Scholfield Barracks, Wheeler Field, Territory of Hawaii in April 1929. This ceremony is illustrated in Figure 21. Both men were members of the Air Service.

Eric Nelson, as a First Lieutenant Air Service, had previously been awarded the Distinguished Service Medal by Act of Congress in 1925, (G.O. No. 14, 1925 citation not obtained). His DFC was presented to him at a review of the 6th Engineers at Fort Lawton, Washington. Lieutenant Nelson had also been one of four airmen to finish in the Douglas World Cruise starting in April 1924. Only one plane had completed the full circuit, with the crew of Lieutenants Leslie Arnold and Lowell Smith. Smith was also a later DFC winner as discussed in Chapter Three.

Master Sergeant Joseph English, Air Service, became the first enlisted man to receive the DFC from the War Department. His DFC was sent to the Commanding General of Langley Field for presentation. James Long, formerly a Sergeant in the Air Service, was presented his medal without the presence of troops at Fort Ethan Allen, Vermont.

Figure 21: Clarence Crumrine as 1st Lieutenant, after his receipt of the DFC for the Alaska air-mapping expedition. This ceremony took place at Schofield Barracks, Territory of Hawaii.
National Archives and Records Administration

Medals were approved August 18, 1928, and presented on various dates at various locations in the United States and Hawaii as discussed above.

Name	Dates Award	Presentation	No. Award	Medal
Capt. St. Clair Street	08-18-28	10-08-28	25	(26)[2]
1st Lt. Ross C. Kirkpatrick	08-18-28	04-19-29(post)	26	32
1st Lt. Clifford C. Nutt	08-18-28	04-04-29	27	36
2nd Lt. Clarence E. Crumrine	08-18-28	04-16-29	28	37
1st Lt. Eric H. Nelson	08-18-28	08-06-29	29	34
MSgt. Joseph E. English	08-18-28	06-25-29	30	33
Sgt. James D. Long	08-18-28	04-11-29	31	35

Saint Clair Street served in World War I, commanding Field 5 in the Third Aviation Centre of the A.E.F.. He was promoted to Major General in World War II, and commanded the 13th Air Force under Lieutenant General George C. Kenney in MacArthur's South West Pacific Area (SWPA) as noted for General Whitehead in Chapter One. The 13th supported the Philippine operations after the invasion, and incorporated some Marine Corps units. It headquartered on Leyte in 1945 in support of the Eighth Army, where Street was later relieved by Major General Paul B. Wurtsmith. St. Clair Street, Jr. graduated from West Point 1949 and retired as Lieutenant Colonel.

Balloon Flight Heroism. Per WD GO No. 14, Uzal Girard Ent was awarded the DFC for Heroism for action on May 30, 1928. It is interesting to note that both the first (Hawthorne Gray) and second War Department awards for heroism were for balloon flights. Lieutenant Ent, Air Corps, was serving as aide to Lieutenant Paul Evert in the 1928 National Balloon Race, when their balloon was struck by lightning or a severe charge. Evert was killed, the balloon set afire, and Ent severely shocked. Ent attempted to revive the pilot, then maneuvered the balloon away from habitation and stayed with it while afire and crashing rather than parachute to safety. The Assistant Secretary of War Davison presented him his DFC on June 25, 1929 at Langley Field. His award had been announced in the New York Times datelined September 15, 1928, as "HERO IN BALLOON RACE TO WEAR FLYING CROSS."

He was later awarded the decoration and diploma of the Condor of the Andes in the grade of Officer, September 1941 for ferrying the remains of a Bolivian Officer from Washington, D.C. to Bolivia. In WWII he became a Brigadier General, and as head of the 9th Bomber Command, led the first Ploesti oil fields attack. His awards include the DSC (twice) DSM (twice), Legion of Merit, a second DFC, and two Air Medals. Ent had been a Sergeant in a balloon company in 1919 when he was appointed to West Point from which he graduated in 1924 and later trained as both lighter- and heavier-than-air pilot. His son, Uzal Wellington Ent, was admitted to West Point in 1949 but did not graduate.

Name	Dates		No.	
	Award	Presentation	Award	Medal
2nd Lt. Uzal G. Ent	09-11-28	06-25-29	32	30

AWARDS TO THE UNITED STATES NAVY

First Naval Officer Flight to Hawaii. The Dole Airplane Race to Hawaii was described in the War Department Awards section, under the award to pilot Arthur Goebel. On August 16, 1927, the aircraft *Woolaroc* won the air race from San Francisco to Hawaii to win a prize offered by the Dole Company. The aircraft was navigated by U.S. Navy Lieutenant William Davis, Jr. of Savannah. The citation read (in part): "For extraordinary achievement ...and in recognition of his courage, skill, and resourcefulness as navigator of the plane *Woolerac* which won the Dole air race.... He took part in this hazardous undertaking voluntarily in the interest of the development of aerial navigation, and became the first Naval Aviator to reach the Hawaiian Islands from the Mainland by air."

Navy award No. 6 was made May 9, 1928. Davis received the cross on the same date as Lieutenant Cornwall, in Pensacola, Florida, August 31, 1929. See Chapter One for New York Times article about presentation. Colonel Arthur Goebel, U.S. Army Air Corps was pilot of the plane. Davis, by then a Lieutenant Commander, became Officer in Charge of an Aircraft Armament Unit at Naval Air Station, Norfolk for testing armament systems, on June 11, 1941.

Name	Dates		Medal
	Award	Presentation	No.
6. Lt. William Virginius Davis, Jr.	05-09-28	08-31-29	tbd

AWARDS TO THE U.S. MARINE CORPS

Miami to Managua Flight January 14, 1928. Major Louis M. Bourne was cited for his achievements in piloting a Fokker TA-1-7562 across the Gulf of Mexico to Nicaragua and, while there, assuming command of 2nd Brigade Aircraft Squadrons where he "...displayed Skill, Daring, and Leadership under most Trying and Hazardous Conditions." His early USMC serial number was 097. Major Bourne's DFC was found behind a business in Julian, California, c. 1980. The finder succeeded in placing it with an historian, who arranged that it be donated to the USMC Museum Branch at Quantico, VA where it now resides.

7. Maj. Louis M. Bourne   Dates tbd   Medal no. 59

Nicaragua Bandit Attack Award. After three enlistments, starting July 6, 1912, and nine years in the USMC, Michael Wodarczyk was discharged in order to accept appointment as Marine Gunner, on August 19, 1921. In 1923 he was detailed as student Naval Aviator. While on duty in San Diego he was ordered to Nicaragua. He was involved in the Attack on Ocotal on July 16, 1927 with Lt. Boyden's patrol, and recommended for a DFC by Major Rowell who was involved in the same action as described in Chapter One.

The DFC was not approved but he was given a commendation by the Secretary of the Navy dated January 16, 1928. His recommendation had stated, "(Wodarczyk) while piloting a plane in Lt. Boyden's patrol, he was the first to discover the attack on Ocotal. Later the same day he piloted a plane in the formation that drove the bandits from Ocotal. He has participated in 22 contacts with hostile outlaws, his planes have been hit by hostile fire 15-20 times and his skill and courage have been outstanding in all engagements." If this DFC had been awarded, he would have been the third USMC DFC winner after Rowell and Boyden.

"24 February, 1928 - Appointed CMG (Chief Marine Gunner) a (commission) to rank with but after 2nd Lieutenant." Four days later he was recommended for a DFC again for February 28, 1928 actions while "Piloting an OC-1 on a courier mission, Wodarczyk landed at Ocotal Nicaragua and was notified that a Marine pack train was being attacked... about 30 miles away. Although his plane had no front gun, he loaded his plane with bombs, and proceeded immediately to the assistance of the besieged party. Upon his arrival at the scene of the attack he found that the outlaws had been driven off by a relief column of our troops. He at once went in search of the outlaws, and near Pijanal village, he observed a party hiding in a barn. For positive identification he flew very low over the building and was met by a heavy burst of rifle fire which severe y damaged his plane and narrowly missed hitting the pilot. With no front gun and the plane's tail partly shot away, (he) single-handed attacked - with great skill and exceptional courage. He splendidly place{d} bombs - from a dangerously low altitude, killed the outlaw chief... and completely dispersed the hostile group."

Sgt. Wodarczyk held a Mexican Campaign Medal and, for World War I, Medaille Militaire, Croix de Guerre with Gold Star and also one with Palm, Victory medal and Wound and War Certificates, Nicaraguan Ribbon with Star, plus the Santo Domingo Expeditionary Ribbon.

8. CMG Michael Wodarczyk   Presented 09-07-28   Medal no. tbd

He was presented his DFC in the same ceremony with his former Squadron Commander, Major Rowell, who had first recommended him for the DFC for Ocotal. See Chapter One for photograph.

The three other pilots shared a common citation: "...operating in Nicaragua on January 14, 1928, during an attack against a strong force of bandits under General Sandine occupying a prepared position on Chipote Mountain the force... attacked the position and persisted in the face of heavy rifle and machine gun fire until the bandits were put to flight after suffering from the effects of well directed aircraft fire. The defeat was of great importance... as it resulted in many of the bandits fleeing across the frontier to Honduras."

Name	Dates Award	Presentation	Medal No.
9. 1st Lt. Frank H. Lamson-Scribner	04-14-1930	tbd	tbd
10. 1st Lt. Frank B. Weir	04-14-1930	tbd	tbd
11. Master Tech. Sgt. Albert S. Munsch	04-14-1930	tbd	tbd

The careers of Frank Lamson-Scribner and Frank Weir ran in close parallel. Lamson-Scribner, from Washington, D.C., and Weir, from Brooklyn, entered the Naval academy in 1919 and were commissioned Marine Second Lieutenants in June 1923. Both went to Quantico, Virginia then to Puerto Rico. They both entered flight training in 1926, and were both assigned to Nicaragua as Naval Aviators. In World War II Lamson-Scribner saw service in Alaska being awarded the combat "V" for service on Attu, then saw service in the Ellice Islands, Tarawa, and Marshall and Gilbert Islands. He was promoted to Brigadier General in 1951, then Major General, retired. He died March 27, 1985 in Charleston, SC. Weir saw service at Guadalcanal-Tulagi, Russell Islands, New Georgia, Vella Lavella, Treasury-Bouganville and Cape Toroklina in WWII and was promoted to Brigadier/Major General, retired, 1952. He died September 17, 1989 (at El Toro, California?).

General Weir was also awarded the Legion of Merit, Bronze Star, 2nd Nicaraguan, American Defense Service (Base), Asiatic-Pacific (1 Silver and 1 Bronze Star), American Area, WWII Victory, and China Service Medals. He was also awarded the Nicaraguan Ribbon with Star, and the China Breast Order of the Cloud and Banner.

A summary of this time period reflects eighteen War Department awards in 1928, of which at least three were not presented until 1929. The single Naval award was not presented until 1929. Finally, there were five Marine Corps awards, of which at least three were... probably not presented until 1930.

[1] Parentheses indicate that the number is not known but fits the sequence and dates of these entries.

[2] Number unknown, possible number inserted due to sequence of awards. However medal numbers are usually missing from data available to the author at this point. Furthermore some numbered medals ordered by the War Department were sent to the Navy for USMC or USN personnel. Consequently, unconfirmed numbers will not be noted in the book hereafter.

CHAPTER THREE
FLIGHT TESTING AND EXPEDITIONS 1929

GENERAL

The Antarctic expedition of Commander Richard E. Byrd achieved its record-breaking goal of flight over the South Pole in 1929. Though sounding relatively simple today, the expedition required two ships, three aircraft and over 80 men for a two-year period.

Lieutenant T. G. W. Settle with Ensign W. Bushnell, U.S. Navy, won the National Balloon Race and Litchfield Trophy this year. They established long-distance world records in three categories, and became eligible for the next International race. Another Navy win was by Lieutenant W. G. Tomlinson, securing the Curtiss Marine Trophy for speed at 162.5 mph. The city of Miami inaugurated an airfield and an aviation show that became famous, as well as a training ground for such military pilots as Claire Chennault.

Four British pilots flew the *Southern Cross* from Australia to London, 12,000 miles, in 12 days and 21 hours. Four Russian pilots covered 13,300, miles, Moscow to New York via Seattle, with 142 flying hours. The *Graf Zeppelin* traveled around the world in 21 days, at speeds up to 70 miles per hour. The majority of Distinguished Flying Cross awards were made for flight test activities.

There is an interesting article in the New York Times, September 2, 1929, about two men whose awards are described in this chapter, James Doolittle, Army, and Alford Williams, Navy, for an air show also including Charles Lindbergh and his formation group, "The High Hats". Doolittle lost his wings in a dive pull-out, and had to bail out at 2,000 feet. Next Williams flew a Navy Seahawk with a special carburetor allowing inverted flight. He performed an outside loop within 1,000 feet of the ground and came down to within three feet of the ground, inverted. After a steep vertical climb, as he hung almost motionless, he flipped over, half rolled to upright position, and fishtailed, landing gently right in front of the stands. At this point, Lindbergh's team flew many maneuvers at twenty-five feet or less of separation. Doolittle next flew again and power-dived almost as sharply as when he lost his wings less than an hour before, and climaxed the show with barrel rolls and combination actions!

AWARDS BY THE U.S. WAR DEPARTMENT

Spitzbergen Flight. Carl Ben Eielson, Air Corps Reserve, made a long range Alaska Flight April 15-16, 1928, as recorded in WD GO No. 3, 1929. Lieutenant Eielson was well known in his day for various exploits. These include the first Alaskan airmail flight, and first airplane flight over the continent of Antarctica in December 1928, spending ten flight hours exploring and mapping 100,000 square miles. Both this flight and the Alaska flight were in conjunction with the noted British explorer Captain George H. Wilkins, later known as Sir Hubert Wilkins. According to the New York Times, datelined December 9, 1928 the Secretary of War Davis announced that Eielson was awarded the DFC for "EXTRAORDINARY ACHIEVEMENT" in an aerial flight. "Lieutenant Eielson as pilot was accompanied by Captain George H. Wilkins...from Point Barrow, Alaska to Dead Man's Island, Archipelago of Spitzbergen. The flight covered 2,200 miles over the arctic without stop. The severity of the weather, the storm area through which they passed, the impossibility of safe landing en route, with no hope of aid in case of forced landing, and the complete success of the enterprise, distinguishes this as one of the most extraordinary aerial achievements in history" reads the citation.

Eielson had previously been a winner of the prestigious Harmon Trophy and was also recognized by the Ligue Internationale des Aviateurs of Paris in 1929.

Name	Dates		No.	
	Award	Presentation	Award	Medal
1st Lt. Carl B. Eielson	12-09-28	tbd	(33)	tbd

The First Powered Flight. The Wright Brothers were retroactively recognized for their flight of December 17, 1903. On February 27, 1929 Orville Wright, and Wilbur Wright (posthumously), were honored for their pioneer flight at Kitty Hawk and major contributions to aviation, by the presentation of the DFC. Figure 22 shows the presentation to Orville at the War Department in Washington, D.C. Orville was presented with his own and Wilbur's medals, their certificates and citations at this time.

Name	Dates		No.	
	Award	Presentation	Award	Medal
Wilbur Wright	12-18-28	(to Orville)	34	none
Orville Wright	12-18-28	02-27-29	(35)	none

Wood and Canvas Heroes

Figure 22: Secretary of War, Dwight Davis presents Orville Wright, center, with his DFC. Orville also received Wilbur's posthumous DFC. Assistant Secretary for aviation, F. Trubee Davison is at left. This ceremony was held February 27, 1929.
Library of Congress

These awards were included in WD GO No. 7, 1929 with those for the refueling flight described below. Information and photos from the Special Collections Department at the Wright State University Libraries in Dayton, Ohio show that the Wright brothers, medals in their collections have engraved names of each brother, with BB & B/Bronze hallmark but with no number, as seen in Figure 23.

Refueling Flight of 150 Hours. On January 1st through 7th 1929, four pilots and a crewman participated in a grueling 150 plus hours of continuous flight, including in-flight refueling. According to the New York Times article headlined "Question Mark Crew get Flying Crosses: Eaker to Add Oak Leaves to

Flight Testing and Expeditions

Figure 23: Reverse of Wright Brothers medals, showing standard naming and BB&B Bronze hallmark but no number.
Wright University Library Collection

Earlier Award." General Order No. 7, 1929, includes the award of four DFC's and of the first ever Distinguished Flying Cross Oak Leaf Cluster (second award) to Captain Ira C. Eaker for the same flight project. See Chapter One for his original award. Spaatz commanded the flight experiment, conducted in the *Question Mark* endurance aircraft. The crew is shown with their aircraft in Figure 24.

Figure 24: Crew of the *Question Mark* aerial refueling flight with their plane. From left; Carl Spaatz, Ira Eaker, Harry Halverson, Elwood Quesada, and Ray Hook.
San Diego Aerospace Museum

"Spaatz, Quesada and Hook were presented their medals by Secretary of War Davis in Washington, D.C. in his office this afternoon" (March 2), according to the Times. All men were in the U.S. Army Air Corps. The article quoted the citation for Major Spaatz (sic) as being for extraordinary achievement: "...By his endurance, resourcefulness, and leadership, he demonstrated future possibilities in aviation which were heretofore not appreciated...." Citations were mailed to Spaatz and to Quesada March 30, 1929.

At the time of the presentation, Eaker was enroute from Seattle to Kelly Field, Texas for a March 10 Dawn-to-Dusk flight attempt to Panama. His certificate was mailed to him March 29, 1929

Flight Testing and Expeditions

and he was presented his Oak Leaf Cluster by the Commanding Officer of Bolling Field in April.

Halverson, stationed at March Field, California, later received his Cross from Brigadier General Foulois in the auditorium at Wright Field.

Name	Dates		No.	
	Award	Presentation	Award	Medal
Maj. Carl Spaatz	03-02-29	03-02-29	37	40
Capt. Ira C. Eaker	03-02-29	04-06-29	OLC #1	
1st Lt. Harry Halverson	03-02-29	07-13-29	38	tbd
2nd Lt./Maj. Elwood R. Quesada	03-02-29	03-02-29	39	38
S/Sgt. Ray W. Hook	03-02-29	03-02-29	(40)	tbd

Carl 'Tooey' Spaatz had won a DSC in the 3rd, (later 13th) Aero Squadron in WWI, was credited with two victories, and was promoted to Major. He became Commanding General of the 8th Air Force in WWII (before Jimmy Doolittle), then commander of the N.W. African Air Force. After VE Day he led the Air Forces that bombed Japan. He was later commander of the U.S. Strategic Air Forces, and later the first Chief of Staff of the U.S. Air Force. Spaatz graduated West Point in 1914 entering the Infantry then Air Service. His other awards include the DSM and the Bronze Star.

Quesada was awarded the diploma of "Military Aviator Honoria Causa" as a member of the military mission to Argentina. He served as a flight commander in the 9th (Tactical) Air Force in WWII and was later Lt. General commanding the Tactical Air Command, United States Air Force.

Awards of WD GO No. 12, 1929

New York City to Columbia, 4,600 Miles. Captain Benjamin Mendez of the Colombian Army made this flight from November

23 to December 30, 1928. The General Order was issued in accord with the Act of Congress approved March 1, 1929 (Private No. 449, by the 70th Congress). He was presented his DFC the evening of March 7, 1930 by the American Minister in Bogota, Columbia.

Oakland, California to Molokai, Hawaii. This 25fi-hour flight by a single pilot, Lt. Ernest Smith, Air Corps Reserve, on July 14 and 15, 1927 only about two months after Lindbergh's and of a comparable difficulty, received little acclaim. The flight lasted about four and one-half hours less than Lindbergh's and was only about 2,400 miles, but was much longer over water. Smith was cited on WD GO No. 12 with Mendez, above. Later, as a Captain, Specialist Reserve, he was presented his cross at Crissy Field in California with ceremony in August 1929.

Name	Dates		No.	
	Award	Presentation	Award	Medal
Capt. Benjamin Mendez	03-01-29	03-07-30	36	22
2nd Lt. Ernest L. Smith	03-06-29	08-15-29	41	tbd

WD GO No. 16, 1929, combined four awards. These were announced in the New York Times, datelined August 1, 1929 under a headline "FOUR ARMY AIRMEN WIN FLYING CROSS". The story describes Lieutenant Doolittle as receiving the principal award "because of receiving both the DFC and the Oak Leaf Cluster," as described later.

Refueling Flight of 1923. Awards were made retroactively to two Air Service pilots who conducted in-flight refueling tests on June 28-29,1923 breaking endurance, speed, and distance records. Lieutenants Smith and Richter flew for 37 hours in tests conducted in California. They established speed records for the range from 2,500 to 5,000 kilometers, and the distance record of 5,300 kilometers. According to the Times, they established the

Flight Testing and Expeditions

practice of in-flight refueling. A New York Times article, datelined November 14, 1929, provided further details on Captain L.H. Smith and Lieutenant Richter. "The presentation [to Smith] was made at Wright Field, Ohio, by Brig. Gen. Benjamin D. Foulois, Chief of the Materiel Division of the Air Corps at that field. Lieutenant John P. Richter - has already received the decoration." The citations were for Extraordinary Achievement, "by their endurance, resourcefulness, and determination, they reflected great credit on themselves and the Army of the United States."

Name	Dates Award	Presentation	No. Award	Medal
1st Lt. Lowell H. Smith	07-02-29	11-04-29	42	64
1st Lt. John P. Richter	07-02-29	03-28-29	43	65

Captain Smith first found fame after he was appointed commander of the Army's eight-man, four-aircraft, around-the-world flight in 1924 after the plane of the original commander (Major Frederick Martin) was damaged in Alaska. Only two aircraft and four men completed the flight; Smith and his co-pilot Lt. Leslie Arnold completed the full circuit to large ovations in Japan, Shanghai, Calcutta, Paris, and London. President Calvin Coolidge waited for their arrival in the rain for three hours at Bolling Field, Washington. Smith was given a triumphant crossing of the United States to the official finish of the first circumnavigation of the world by air, and thence to his home state California. His medal is in the collection of the National Air and Space Museum of the Smithsonian Institute and is shown in Figure 25.

Lieutenants Eric Nelson and John Harding who had a delayed take off eventually also finished the world flight. Nelson's award of the DFC for the Alaska Expedition is written up in Chapter Two. Lowell Smith also held the Distinguished Service Medal.

Figure 25: Reverse of August C. Frank medal number 64, named to Lowell H. Smith, the 42nd War Department award.
National Air and Space Museum

Flight Testing and Expeditions

According to the Times article, Captain Smith, "who had returned several months ago from a three-year tour of the Hawaiian Islands, is stationed at the Curtiss Airplane and Motor plant at Buffalo, where he is the Air Corps representative."

Richter's Award Certificate for the DFC is shown in Figure 26. The size of the original certificate is 12fi by 14fi. Brigadier General Foulois presented his DFC to him in the auditorium at Wright Field, Dayton, Ohio. His DFC and certificate are located in the Airmen Memorial Museum, Suitland, Maryland.

Figure 26: Certificate for award of DFC to John Richter, for Extraordinary Achievement. Original said to be 12 1/2 x 14 1/2 inches.
Airmen Memorial Museum

Florida to California, 1922. First Lieutenant James H. Doolittle, Air Service, made a flight from Florida to California September

4th and 5th, 1922 in less than 23 hours. This flight was cited for distance, covering 2,163 miles with only one stop between Pablo Beach and San Diego. According to the Times, Doolittle's flight had demonstrated the possibility of moving Air Corps units to all parts of the country in twenty-four hours.

Doolittle was simultaneously awarded the Oak Leaf Cluster (second OLC awarded) in the same GO for flight-testing done in 1924 at McCook Field, when he first performed the outside loop. These were tests to gauge what flight loads could be imposed on planes in extreme conditions of air combat, according to the Times article. The citation read in part: "These tests were put through with that fine combination of fearlessness and skill which constitutes the essence of distinguished flying." Doolittle was presented both the DFC and the Oak Leaf Cluster by the Commanding General, 1st Division, Brigadier General H. A. Drum at Fort Hamilton, New York.

Doolittle had received a Doctorate in Aeronautics from the Massachusetts Institute of Technology, which he put to good use in various flight safety studies and experiments. He was very active for years in flight testing as well as competitive racing. In September 1929 Lt. Doolittle flew in the rear seat of a trainer with a canvas cover completely over his cockpit. Using only three instruments, altimeter, horizon indicator, and directional gyro, he took off, climbed, turned 180 degrees and landed within yards of his takeoff spot at Mitchel Field, NY. In the front seat of his airplane, Lt. Ben Kelsey held his hands over his head to show that he never needed to touch the controls.

In 1942, Lieutenant Colonel Doolittle was awarded the Medal of Honor for the famous attack by the bomber group he led on Tokyo in April 1942. This award was presented to him at Washington, D.C. by President Roosevelt, May 19, 1942, at the White House. Doolittle is credited with saving the reputation of

Flight Testing and Expeditions

the B-26 Bomber after many fatal crashes by his aggressive personal flight testing. He later became the Commander of the Eighth Air Force in WWII.

Flight Testing in 1926. Finally, First Lieutenant Harry A. Sutton, Air Corps, Award Number 45, was presented his DFC on August 28, 1929 for flight test activities performed December 15th to the 22nd, 1926 at Santa Monica, California. After Sutton's close friend Lieutenant Barksdale was killed in tailspin research, Sutton took over testing and eventually redesigned the plane to eliminate spinning. In his citation, (according to the New York Times), Air Corps officers attached to the Engineering Division were quoted as calling his achievement, "the finest demonstration of brains, courage, and daring which had been brought to their attention in many years."

Presentation by General Foulois to Sutton was at the same date as Lieutenant Richter, above. Lieutenant Sutton further received the Mackay Trophy in 1928 for his spin testing exploits.

Name	Dates		No.	
	Award	Presentation	Award	Medal
1st Lt./Gen. James H. Doolittle	07-02-29	10-25-29	44	tbd
same - Oak Leaf Cluster	07-02-29	10-25-29	OLC # 2	
1st Lt. Harry A. Sutton	07-02-29	08-28-29	45	tbd

UNITED STATES NAVY AWARDS

Inverted Flight Tests by The Speed King. The DFC was awarded to Lieutenant A. J. Williams in May of 1929. His lengthy citation described his aerial flights of May 10, 1928 in which he "made a study of the action and best methods of control of a violently maneuvered plane - attended by exceedingly great personal risk of life. As a result of his flights and studies, he was able to evolve certain principles and practical application, maneuvers have been made safer, and methods developed for more fully and accurately testing the capabilities of various types of airplanes." Reference was also made to his high-speed flights and to research and writing in the field of aeronautics.

Lieutenant Alford Williams became known as the King of Speed. He finished fourth, behind Lieutenant H. J. Brow in the Pulitzer Trophy race on October 14, 1922 and set two speed records in October 1923. He then achieved a record 266.59 miles per hour at Mitchel Field November 4, a record which lasted into the 1930s. Two days later he climbed to 5,000 feet in 1 minute, beating the previous record of 2,000 feet in the same time. Williams was the 7th naval award. His cross was presented by the Secretary of the Navy.

Two New York Times articles were printed about Williams. A Washington release datelined May 16, 1929 states: "The Distinguished Flying Cross was awarded by the Navy today to Lieutenant A. J. Williams, crack speed pilot, for his achievements in inverted flight at the Anacostia Naval Air Station in March last year, and other distinguished feats in the air. The decoration will be presented to him tomorrow by Secretary Adams." The next article, datelined May 17 states, "Standing before the plane in which he performed many of his exploits, Lieutenant Alford J. Williams, Navy pilot, lawyer, and one-time big league pitcher, received the Distinguished Flying Cross at the Anacostia Naval Air Station today. The decoration was pinned to his uniform coat by Secretary Adams on behalf of President Hoover. Mr. and Mrs. Williams of New York, his father and mother, and their daughter Frances came here for the ceremony." They may be seen in Figure 27.

First Posthumous Naval Award, 1930. George Thomas Cuddihy was awarded the DFC posthumously for his achievements on August 7, 1929 while flight testing the type F4B-1 air-

Flight Testing and Expeditions

Figure 27: Alford J. Williams, center, after his DFC presentation in Washington, D.C., standing in front of his plane. From left, Williams' father, wife, mother and sister. Date is May 17, 1929.
Courtesy of a Private Collector

plane spinning characteristics. "Putting the plane into a tailspin at 10,000 feet, and entering a flat spin apparently not able to be brought under control, Lieutenant Cuddihy discovered a method of altering the head resistance and was able to regain control. This principle of regaining control is one which applies to all types of airplanes and will undoubtedly be the means of preventing many crashes." His citation reads: "Lieutenant Cuddihy's entire service in the aeronautical forces of the Navy has been marked by conscientious hard work and crowned by notable achievements, some of which are his services as a test pilot, as a pilot of racing craft and in successfully making a flight from Buenos Aires, Argentina, to Santiago, Chile over the Andes Mountains. The interest and efficiency displayed by Lieut. Cuddihy in the performance of his duty, and his willingness to undertake the most hazardous feats have contributed much towards the advancement of the science of aeronautics, while his modesty, earnestness, and courage have been an inspiration to his comrades." Cuddihy had set a world speed record of 188.08 mph, October, 1924. The author did not discover the date or cause of death.

Name	Date Award	Presentation	Medal No.
7. Lt. Alford J. Williams	05-16-29	05-17-29	tbd
8. Lt. George Thomas Cuddihy	tbd(posthumous)	03-24-30	tbd

UNITED STATES MARINE CORPS AWARDS

None found.

This Chapter for 1929 lists: Thirteen new DFC awards and two OLC awards by the War Department, and two Naval Awards.

CHAPTER FOUR
RESCUES AND SPECIAL FLIGHTS 1930 & 1931

GENERAL

The prestigious Schneider Trophy races, begun in 1913 for seaplanes, terminated in 1931. The races first won in 1913 by the Frenchman Maurice Provost at a speed of 45.7 mph, ended with John Boothman of Britain winning at an average of 340 mph. Out of 11 winners, there was only one American, James Doolittle in 1925.

Roscoe Turner, a flashy pilot who had just finished pilot training as World War I ended, started to become known for a variety of promotional stunts, wearing an impressive custom uniform. In 1930, he convinced Earl Gilmore of Gilmore Oil Company, that he could enhance his business. Gilmore bought Turner a new Lockheed plane. Turner obtained a lion cub (a lion being the Gilmore logo), and flew with him for over 30,000 miles before Gilmore, the lion, became too big to fly. Turner became a hero to the press, the movie industry, and to the public. Gilmore, the lion, now resides in the Smithsonian.

Clyde Pangburn, a stunt pilot, and co-pilot Hugh Herndon achieved another first, the crossing of the Pacific, from Japan to the state of Washington in 1931. After being detained as spies in Japan, convicted and fined, the two set off for Idaho to set a new long-distance record. Dropping their landing gear after takeoff to reduce drag, they landed in Washington after being unable to achieve Idaho due to fog, and made their planned belly landing. After their flight, the Japanese Consul General presented them with the gold Medal of Merit of the Imperial Aeronautical Society, the same as awarded to Dieudonne Costes as mentioned in Chapter Two.

AWARDS BY THE U.S. WAR DEPARTMENT

On January 28, 1931, the War Department issued their General Orders No. 2., 1931, primarily announcing awards and citations. The initial award, for the Medal of Honor, stated: "Edward V. Rickenbacker, Colonel, Specialist Reserve, then First Lieutenant, 94th Aero Squadron, Aero Service, American Expeditionary Forces: "For conspicuous gallantry and intrepidity above and beyond the call of duty in action against the enemy near Billy, France, September 25, 1918. While on a voluntary patrol over the lines, Lieutenant Rickenbacker attacked 7 enemy planes. Disregarding the odds against him, he dived on them and shot down one of the Fokkers out of control. He then attacked one of the Halberstadts and sent it down also." The Order also rescinded the award of an Oak Leaf Cluster to Rickenbacker's DSC.

Further awards authorized in 1931 under General Orders No. 2 were in two groups:

<u>Two Byrd Expedition Awards.</u> The Richard Byrd Antarctic and South Pole Expeditions in 1928 to 1930 included Army personnel as well as Navy. In 1930 two Air Corps Reserve Officers were recognized for their efforts. Captain Ashley McKinley was cited for extraordinary achievement as aerial photographer in connection with the 1928-1930 Byrd Antarctic expedition. "In the face of the very gravest danger, Capt. McKinley performed his duties in such a manner as to deserve the greatest praise. His flights culminated in the flight with three companions, over

Rescues and Special Flights

the South Pole on November 28 and 29, 1929," according to his citation.

Lieutenant Smith was one of the pilots on numerous flights over the South Pole and was cited similarly for extraordinary achievement. The New York Times, datelined July 3, 1930, stated that F. Trubee Davison, Assistant Secretary of War for Aviation announced the awards at a dinner for Admiral Byrd at Garden City, Long Island and that the decorations would be presented in Washington, D.C. the following week. He also announced the award of the Soldier's Medal to Master Sergeant Benjamin Roth for his role as an Air Corps mechanic during the expedition.

Name	Dates		No.	
	Award	Presentation	Award	Medal
Capt. Ashley C. McKinley	07-03-30	07-09-30	46	73
2nd Lt. Dean Cull Smith	07-03-30	07-09-30	47	72

McKinley (and maybe others?) was also awarded a gold medal by a special Act of Congress (Public Resolution No. 75, 71st Congress) dated May 23, 1930, on behalf of the Navy. A letter from Rear Admiral Byrd to the Assistant Secretary of War F. Trubee Davison cites these men and recommends their DFC award as follows: "Captain McKinley made every flight of exploration undertaken by the expedition in Antarctica, which included the flight to the South Pole, the Eastern flight where new land was discovered and claimed in the name of the United States, the base laying flight to the Queen Maude Range, and the flight across the ice barrier south of Discovery inlet." McKinley was third in command of the expedition.

Dean Smith was also cited in Byrd's letter as he was one of the pilots of the expedition and piloted the Fairchild plane the *Stars and Stripes* while going to the rescue of Dr. Gould and his party after they were marooned in the Rockefeller Mountains. "He showed extraordinary skill, due to which the mission of rescue was successfully accomplished." Dean Smith also made the base laying flight ..."(where his) landing at the base of the mountains was successful. On the return trip there was a forced landing in rough area, and again Smith brought his plane down without injuring it."

In his letter, Byrd also cited Master Sergeant Benjamin Roth, U.S. Air Corps, as senior mechanic of the plane *Floyd Bennett* stating that, "in all flying there was no mechanical failure of the engines, despite the work was done in bitter cold."

Smith had served as an enlisted man in WWI. The Secretary of War presented both him and McKinley with dummy DFC medals (according to the award cards) on July 9. Subsequently, each had his Cross sent to him by Registered Mail August 2, 1930, to "Byrd Antarctic Expedition, c/o Biltmore Hotel, New York."

A New York Times article datelined Washington, July 9, 1930, said, "Pinning the decorations to the breasts of the officers, Secretary (of War) Hurley shook hands with Sergeant Roth and informed him that because the Soldier's Medal was only recently authorized as a peacetime decoration, no design for the actual medal had yet been approved. The Sergeant will receive the medal later." In fact the Secretary badly misstated the facts in that the Soldier's Medal, first authorized in 1927 simultaneously with the DFC, had been awarded from 1927 on. Major General James E. Fechet, Chief of the Air Corps, read the citations. Roth's citation "For Heroism" was also contained in WD GO No. 2, 1931.

Daring Air-Sea Rescue off Hawaii, May 14, 1930. Four Army Air Corps personnel received the DFC for Heroism for activities in air-sea rescue off Maui, Hawaii after an Air Force Bomber fell

Rescues and Special Flights

out of a formation of 16 amphibious planes from 8,000 feet, the crew bailing out into the ocean just after 11:00 am. Observing the accident, the airmen, then on a flight from Luke Field to Hilo, immediately acted to effect a rescue. As pilot, Lieutenant Jones (later Captain) landed his plane in very rough and windy seas, his Radioman, Lt. Meyer sent out an SOS. As they attempted rescue, their engine began missing, and finally stopped. Despite Meyer crawling out onto the wing, they were unable to reach any of the downed men owing to the force of the wind, the waves, and the missing motor. Pilot Rawlings (Air Corps Reserve) and his mechanic Sgt. Summers, 4th Observation Squadron, also landed and experienced similar problems. However the SOS and the visual sighting of the aircraft on the ocean, allowed a Navy seaplane to locate and perform rescues of the downed airmen. The rescuers were subsequently in frequent danger while attempting to secure ropes from a Navy tender that arrived on the scene. Consequently, they were not themselves taken off until after 1:00 am the following morning.

Major General William Lassiter, Commanding General, Hawaii Department, presented the medals to the three commissioned Officers in October at Luke Field in Hawaii. A New York Times article, October 30, states: "A parade of troops and an aerial review concluded the ceremony. Sergeant Robert F. Summers, formerly of Luke Field, who also figured in the Maui incident, will receive similar honors at his present main and station," according to the article. Major General Malin Craig, C.G. 9th Corps Area, presented Sergeant Summers his DFC at the Presidio, San Francisco, December 1930.

Name	Dates		No.	
	Award	Presentation	Award	Medal
1st Lt. Ulysses G. Jones	09-05-30	10-30-30	48	tbd
1st Lt. Walter T. Meyer	09-05-30	10-30-30	49	tbd
2nd Lt. Edwin W. Rawlings	09-05-30	10-30-30	50	tbd
Staff Sgt. Robert F. Summers	09-05-30	12-19-30	51	tbd

Ulysses Grant Jones, Jr. graduated West Point in 1942, served at Hq. 32nd Div. in the Pacific Theater in WWII, and retired as Colonel in 1972.

WD General Orders No. 6, 1931 - Secret Mission. On October 11, 1931 two pursuit planes were ordered to make all speed on a secret mission from Newark, New Jersey to Vancouver, British Columbia and return. The War Department issued orders that documents of a secret nature were to be picked up no later than October 15 and delivered to the War Department at New Jersey no later than October 18. Lieutenants Woodring, Air Corps, as leader, and Caldwell, Reserve, were chosen to fly two pursuit aircraft with maximal speed (but minimal blind flying capability).

According to the citations: "Extremely hazardous flying conditions were encountered in Wyoming, snow and sleet destroying all visibility from the ground to 16,000 feet. Lieutenant Caldwell remained with his flight leader until the total lack of visibility caused a separation between them, and he crashed to earth at 2:15 pm, October 15, 1930, and was killed. Lieutenant Woodring arrived back at Newark at 7:00 pm, October 16, 1930 and delivered the document which was the Japanese instrument of ratification of the Navy treaty." The mission and the citations were written up in the New York Times under a dateline of Washington, March 19, 1931.

Name	Dates		No.	
	Award	Presentation	Award	Medal
2nd Lt. William W. Caldwell (posthumous)	03-12-31	05-01-31	52	tbd
2nd Lt. Irvin A. Woodring	03-12-31	04-16-31	53	tbd

Both awards were for heroism; Caldwell's medal was presented posthumously to his father, F. G. Caldwell at the Presidio, San Francisco, May 1. Woodring had been presented his award in

Rescues and Special Flights

April at Rockwell Field, California by Major General Malin Craig, Commanding 9th Corps Area.

UNITED STATES NAVY AWARDS

High Altitude Flight Testing and Records Award. Lieutenant Apollo Soucek carried out high-altitude experiments, and on May 8, 1929, he established a world's record for heavier-than-air aircraft at 39,140 feet for which he was awarded the DFC. He was flying a Wright Apache with a 425-hp Pratt and Whitney engine, over Anacostia, Maryland. On June 4 he set the world record for a seaplane at 38,560 feet. Soucek's citation "For Extraordinary Achievement in the art of high altitude flying..." noted the development of engines, propellers, oxygen and other flying equipment as well as prestige for American Aviation. He is listed as U.S. Navy award No. 9. On the first anniversary of his record flight, Soucek flew a Wright Apache now with a 450-hp engine to a new record altitude of 43,166 feet. and regained the world record which he had lost. Soucek is shown leaving his plane after his exploit in Figure 28.

The ceremony of presentation was held at North Island, San Diego, California. The Commander Aircraft Squadrons, Battle Fleet, Admiral J.M. Reeves, presented the DFC to Soucek. Figure 29 shows this ceremony, including Soucek and CRE Alexander (described below). Apollo Soucek, as a Captain, became the first commanding officer of the carrier *Franklin Delano Roosevelt*, commissioned in October 1945. As Rear Admiral, Soucek was chief of BuAer 1953-55. In researching this book, a naval aviator in the same pre-WWII period was noted, who would certainly seem to have been Apollo's brother. His name was Lieutenant Zeus Soucek. Perhaps the parents wanted offspring from A to Z. Zeus had participated in many record flights in 1928 for aircraft duration and load carrying records.

9. Lt. Apollo Soucek Presentation 12-20-30, Medal No. tbd

Figure 28: Apollo Soucek leaves his Apache Seaplane after setting altitude record of 39,140 feet, May 8, 1929.
National Air and Space Museum

Awards for 1926 Alaskan Aerial Survey Expedition - 1930.
The Alaska Survey expedition for which Lieutenant Wyatt was awarded the DFC, (Chapter One), later resulted in seven more awards for surveys conducted in 1926 and recommended May 31, 1929.

Rescues and Special Flights

Figure 29: Lieutenant A. Soucek, left, and Chief Radio Electrician C. G. Alexander with their just presented DFCs from the Battle Fleet Aircraft Squadron, December 20, 1930.
National Archives and Records Administration

Name	Dates Award	Presentation	Medal No.
10. Lt. Wallace M. Dillon		11-29-30	tbd
11. Lt. Eugene F. Burkett	06-09-30[1]		tbd
12. Lt. Cdr. Richard F. Whitehead	06-09-30	11-29-30	tbd
13. CRe Claude George Alexander	06-09-30	12-20-30	tbd[1]
14. CPh Patrick Andrew McDonough	06-09-30	11-29-30	tbd[1]
15. CAP Thomas George Reid (Postumous)	06-09-30	11-29-30	tbd[1]
16. Ph1C William Joseph Murtha	06-09-30	11-29-30	tbd[1]

The citation data seen for members of the above group note their achievement in participating in and aiding in the successful, hazardous and difficult aerial survey. The citation data furnished to the author states for extraordinary achievement. Figure 30 is a photograph of Lieutenant Dillon. The Navy ordered Dillon's citation to be engraved on his DFC as follows:[2]

> "Lieut. Wallace M. Dillon, U.S.N. For extraordinary achievement while participating in an aerial flight as executive officer and second in command of the Alaskan Aerial Expedition during the summer of 1926, materially aiding in successfully performing a hazardous and difficult aerial survey of Southeastern Alaska".

The same citations and required engravings, with changes in name and assignment were seen for the other men, (except that no data were found for McDonough). This would represent a lot of fine engraving work. Navy Secretary Adams made five presentations to Alaskan pilots 11-29-30, concurrent with that of Antarctic pilot Harold June as noted below, at Anacostia Naval Air Station. These presentations include Dillon, Whitehead, Murtha, McDonough, and, posthumously, to Reid's mother of New York. Alexander was presented with Lieutenant Soucek as noted above. Burkett's presentation is unknown. The actual award sequence is unknown, officers presumably first and in

Rescues and Special Flights

Figure 30: Lieutenant W. M. Dillon, USN liaison officer for the Alaska expedition of 1926.
Courtesy of a private collector

order of seniority which seems to be reasonably as listed. The three Chiefs would also probably have been in order of seniority but are given alphabetically.

With Wyatt in command, Dillon served as Executive Officer. Burkett was Navigator for the expedition and Whitehead the Photographic Officer. The other functions provided were by Chief Radio Electrician Alexander, Chief Photographer McDonough, Pilot Reid, and Photograher Murtha.

Byrd's First Antarctic Expedition Awards 1930. The newly promoted Rear Admiral Richard E. Byrd with a crew of three others, departed New York November 28, 1929 arriving at Little America that night, then flying to the South Pole the following morning. As discussed in Chapter One, the crew consisted of Bernt Balchen, pilot, Chief Aviation Pilot (CAP) Harold Irving June, co-pilot and radio operator, and Captain Ashley C. McKinley (USAS) photographer. Byrd carried a stone from Floyd Bennett's grave that he dropped at the South Pole.

CAP June was presented the DFC as U.S. Navy award No.17, on the first anniversary of his flight, in November 1930 by Secretary of the Navy Adams in a ceremony with a number of Alaskan expedition airmen as described above. June served as relief pilot on the flight made under difficult flying conditions (that) reached the South Pole. The November 29 edition of the New York Times carelessly stated, "Byrd Pilot Will Get Navy Cross Today." The Times goes on to name five airmen of the Alaskan aerial expedition of 1926 receiving the DFC, at the same ceremony. Captain McKinley, Air Corps, was awarded the DFC in July 1930 by the War Department as also covered in this chapter.

Rescues and Special Flights

Name	Dates		Medal
	Award	Presentation	No.
17. CAP Harold Irving June	tbd	11-29-30	tbd

A 'Lost' Award - c. 1930. Lieutenant Commander J. M. Shoemaker, as Captain, became Commanding Officer of the Carrier Franklin, commissioned in January 1944. Shoemaker was apparently given his award for an activity in 1927. Assigned award No. 18 in this listing, data as to the citation and dates have not been located.

18. Lieut. Commander J. M. Shoemaker - no available data

In 1927, Shoemaker was commanding officer of the experimental DF Squadron 2B, designated to test the feasibility of using enlisted pilots with fleet squadrons. The squadron was manned by 4 Naval aviators (Commissioned), and 10 Aviation Pilots (Enlisted), at San Diego, California.

UNITED STATES MARINE CORPS

Antarctic Flight with Byrd. Captain Alton N. Parker, USMC, was pilot of the plane *Floyd Bennett* during much of the exploration of the Antarctic. In particular, on December 5, 1929 he was pilot during discovery of a great new land 300 miles east of Little America which were claimed for the United States, and of a north-south mountain range on the border of the Ross Sea. According to his citation, "Captain Parker in piloting the plane throughout the flight, again demonstrated his exceptional ability as a pilot, and showed a high degree of courage in flying far from base, over water and ice, where in places it was apparent that a forced landing would have meant disaster." The recommendation was submitted August 6, 1930 from Byrd to the SecNav, and was approved by the Navy Awards Board in October 1930.

"Parker was the representative of the Marine Corps Reserve on the expedition," according to Byrd. "The exceptional qualifications as a pilot that Captain Parker demonstrated on the North Pole Expedition [also formed by Byrd] led me to select him as a member of the Antarctic Expedition and pilot for the flight of exploration over the unexplored regions to the Eastward of King Edward VII Land."

**12. Capt. Alton N. Parker, Award 10-23-30,
Presented tbd, Medal No. tbd**

The 1930 Nicaraguan Campaign. Five pilots were awarded the DFC for distinguished service, according to the recommendation for Lieutenant Hart by his Commanding Officer R. J. Mitchell. Use of the term "Distinguished Service" is seen as rare, instead of the nearly universal term, "for Extraordinary Achievement." However, the wording may have been changed on his official citation. The statement reads: "He displayed constant courage and skill while flying over rugged mountainous jungle where a forced landing meant disaster, if not death under most trying conditions of wind and weather. In attacks on hostile bandits he was fearless and eager. His services in maintaining liaison with ground patrols, in carrying freight and passengers, sick and wounded, were untiring and extraordinary."

It is expected that all five pilots would have had similar wording on their citations, which included two engagements: the first when six airplanes attacked bandits on Jicote Mountain on May 2, 1930, and the second when six airplanes attacked and routed a group of bandits estimated at two hundred to six hundred under Sandino, on Saraguasa Mountain, June 19, 1930. On the latter occasion rifle and machine gun fire was met and returned at low altitude over extremely rugged country and in bad weather, in a most valiant and courageous manner. Endorsed March 5, 1931 by the Brigade Commander, it is assumed that all of these awards were made effective the same date. Actual sequence would probably be by rank and seniority. Mitchell, of course, would have been recommended by a higher command.

Name	Dates		Medal
	Award	Presentation	No.
13. Major Ralph J. Mitchell	tbd	tbd	tbd
14. Capt. Byron F. Johnson	tbd	tbd	tbd
15. 1st Lt. John S. E. Young	tbd	01-23-32	tbd
16. 1st Lt. Charles L. Fike	1930?	tbd	tbd
17. 2nd Lt. John N. Hart	03-05-31	01-23-32	tbd

Ralph Mitchell, who led the six plane attack on June 19, graduated from the Naval Academy 1915 and became a naval aviator in 1921. In WWII he was Commander of Aircraft, Solomon Islands, where he planned and executed air actions against Rabaul in New Britain, Bougainville, Green Islands, New Hanover, New Ireland and adjacent waters. He later directed air support operations in the Philippines. His other awards include DSM, Navy and Army, and Legion of Merit with Gold Star. He retired as a Lieutenent General and died May 31, 1970 (Cherry Point, NC?).

Captain Johnson was in command of a two plane patrol which participated in attacking the bandits in the morning and again in the afternoon of June 19. Lieutenent Young was in Johnson's patrol.

Charles Laird Fike was involved in attacks on May 2 and June 19. He also graduated from Annapolis and was commissioned in June 1924. He served on carriers and at fields in China, Guam and Hawaii, where he was Commanding Officer of Squadron 21 on December 7, 1941. He later served at Guadalcanal where he was awarded the DSM as Commanding Officer of the forward echelon at Henderson Field. During August 20 to 30, 1942, units under his command destroyed 21 enemy bombers, 39 Zero type fighters, 2 seaplanes, 3 destroyers, 1 light cruiser, and 1 transport. Other awards include the Bronze Star, Expeditionary, 2nd Nicaraguan, Asiatic-Pacific and WWII Victory. He served in the Bureau of Aeronautics, postwar and retired as Brigadier General. He died from an auto accident in May 1950 and was buried in Arlington.

John Neely Hart, Annapolis 1925, became an aviator in August 1928. He was involved in the same May and June attacks as Fike. He saw action in China and Nicaragua. In WWII he served in the New Hebrides, Guadalcanal, and Southern Solomons being awarded the Legion of Merit with combat. He had been at sea enroute from Hawaii to San Diego on December 7, 1941. Hart died November 14, 1970, (probably at Alexandria, Virginia) as a retired Major General. The presentations to Young and Hart are seen in Figure 31.

Figure 31: First Lieutenants J. N. Hart, left, and J. S. E. Young with their just presented DFCs at Naval Air Station Pensacola, Florida, January 23, 1932.
National Archives and Records Administration

Rescues and Special Flights

Omaha to Anacostia Flight. Captain Arthur H. Page made a pioneer flight from Omaha, Nebraska to Anacostia, D.C. July 1, 1930. Captain Page was piloting an O2U from a sealed and hooded cockpit. The flight route was via Chicago and Cleveland. Lieutenant V. M. Guymon acted as safety pilot, but took over the controls only for the landings after Page had brought the plane over the fields at 200 feet altitude.

18. Captain Arthur H. Page, citation and dates were not located, and no medal number was available.

Previous to his DFC award winning flight, Captain Page was the winner of the last Curtiss Marine Trophy Race on May 31, 1930, while flying an F6C-3 Curtiss at 164 mph. The race was held over the Potomac off Anacostia Naval Air Station.

Captain Page was subsequently entered in the Thompson race, and was the only military entry in 1930. On September 1, while flying an experimental F6C-6, he achieved and increased an early lead. However, on the 17th of 20 laps he crashed to his death, a victim of carbon monoxide.

For the years 1930-31 there were a total of eight War Department awards, ten Navy Department awards to naval personnel, and seven to U.S. Marine Corps pilots as listed in this chapter.

---

[1] Medal numbers 79, 86, 89 and 90 were probably awarded to Alexander, McDonough, Reid and Murtha but the sequence is unknown.

[2] A Navy memo for ordering engraving on medals for Soucek, Dillon, Burkett, Whitehead and Alexander, was dated 10-27-30.

CHAPTER FIVE
HEROISM, NOTED CIVILIANS AND DEVELOPMENTS 1932 - 1934

GENERAL

In Britain, the architect and Member of Parliament Alfred C. Bossom, whose wife and son were killed in an airplane crash at Farnham, England, stated he was negotiating to buy about one half an acre of the farmland where they died as a burial site. A new fast airline service opened on June 11, 1933 across the United States. The New York Times stated; "The fastest schedule ever...went into operation. The planes were on time and the traffic heavy. Eastbound, eighty-three passengers came into Newark on United Airlines new twin-engined, three-mile-a-minute planes, four extra planes being required to carry the travelers. Westbound, seventy-one passengers left for Chicago or beyond."

In July 1933, a New Jersey surgeon Albert Forsythe and his co-pilot Charles Anderson made the first transcontinental flight by black pilots. They spanned 4,000 miles, stopping at some 50 regular and makeshift landing spots enroute.

Ensign Kennett L. Rawson was cited for his activities with the Byrd Antarctic Expedition II in 1934. He was awarded the Navy Cross for his exploits. He served as navigator, and managed to save the *SS Bear of Oakland* from getting frozen into the ice, navigated the trip to Grace McKinley Mountain, and all flights in November and December 1934.

The Army announced plans to resume flights carrying airmail previously stopped after some 11 fatalities. General Foulois announced over NBC that hazards would be reduced by elimination of certain routes, and by eliminating combat equipment while adding flight safety equipment. This was reported in the New York Times March 18, 1934.

WAR DEPARTMENT AWARDS

WD General Orders No. 2 and No. 6 in 1932 - Two awards.

Mid-Air Collision. On December 22, 1931, First Lieutenant Robert D. Moor, Army Air Corps, was awarded the DFC for HEROISM for an event of August 23, 1931. While leading a formation flight, the airplane of a formation-mate, flying on his flank was thrown by a terrific air current into the airplane piloted by Lieut. Moor, disabling the tail group of the latter's airplane and causing it to become almost entirely uncontrollable. Ignoring the opportunity to save himself, Lieutenant Moor endeavored first to save his passenger, and repeatedly ordered him to jump. The passenger eventually jumped and landed safely with parachute, but in so doing unbalanced the airplane which immediately fell out of control, crashed to the ground and burst into flames, resulting in Lieutenant Moor's death and the destruction of the airplane. The circumstances under which Moor sacrificed his life in an effort to save the life of his companion furnished an outstanding example of the loyalty and the heroism which characterize the traditions of the military service.

Moor's DFC award was made for heroism, posthumously. His medal was presented to Mrs. Agnes Moor, guardian of Moor's minor daughter and next of kin, Alice Katherine Moor. The Commanding General, 5th Coast Artillery, made the presentation at Fort Hayes. Moor was also named to the Cheney Award for heroism and humanitarianism for 1931.

Lighter-than-Air Aircraft Incident. Sergeant Frank D. Neff, 2nd Balloon Company, Air Corps, was awarded the DFC for HEROISM on March 31, 1932. Neff was participating in an aerial flight on the night of December 3, 1931, when; "During a severe wind and rain storm, the Army Dirigible TC-71 broke from its moorings as preparations were being made by the crew to start the engines and cast it off to ride out the storm. Sgt. Neff succeeded in getting the right motor started but was unable to start the left motor from within the car. Realizing that the airship was not under full control and in great danger of being wrecked and the crew injured, he immediately discarded his parachute and with complete disregard of his own safety, climbed out of the car onto the unprotected outrigger of the wildly plunging dirigible and, working in the darkness in this perilous position, succeeded in hand-cranking the left motor, thereby bringing the airship under full control. Sgt. Neff's heroic action in risking his life to save the airship from destruction and the crew from injury was in the best traditions of the Air Corps..."

He was listed as the 55th person to receive this War Department Award. The Commanding General Fort Bragg, North Carolina presented Sergeant Neff's DFC to him.

Name	Dates		No.	
	Award	Presentation	Award	Medal
1st Lt. Robert D. Moor	12-22-31	02-06-32 (posthumous)	54	tbd
Sgt. Frank D. Neff	03-31-32	05-26-32	55	tbd

WD General Orders No. 4, 1933 - Civilian Awards. In response to the Act of Congress, Public Resolution 31, approved July 2 and 11, 1932, the War Department issued General Orders for the award of DFCs to five American civilians.

Cross Atlantic Flight in 1930. The most famous person of this group, by today's standards at least, was Amelia Earhart

Putnam the first woman, (and only one, until perhaps recent engagements which the author has not researched,) to be awarded the DFC. Her award was for her May 1932 flight as pilot when she crossed the Atlantic nonstop from Newfoundland to Ireland becoming the second person to cross the Atlantic from west to east in solo flight. This flight succeeded a 1928 cross-Atlantic flight she had made in company with two male pilots, as well as many other record setting flights made by Mrs. Putnam. The 1928 flight, as well as the other exploits, made her famous. Sally Ride, the Space Shuttle astronaut who has been compared to Mrs. Putnam, just recently dedicated a new Goodyear airship, as had Amelia in helping to launch the Goodyear airship *Defender* in 1929.

On this Atlantic flight, she lost her altimeter shortly after takeoff, and guessed at altitude in darkness and fog thereafter. Four hours out of Newfoundland, she saw a cracked weld in the exhaust manifold, which started vibrating after dawn. A gas leak on her reserve tanks became obvious when she switched them on, so she altered her course towards Ireland rather than Paris, and she set down in a convenient cow pasture near Londonderry after she crossed the coast. She became as famous a heroine as Lindbergh had become a hero in this country and abroad, often being referred to as the female "Lindy". Earhart's award, manufactured by BB&B, was presented to her in Los Angeles. Her medal resides in the Libraries Collection at Purdue University, West Lafayette, Indiana.

Vice President Charles Curtis presented Amelia Earhart's DFC to her in the city of Los Angeles. The other four civilian pilots' medals and certificates were presented directly by President Hoover at the White House in Washington. The New York Times article datelined Los Angeles, July 29 (1932) states: "Hoover sends message to Recipient of Congressional Flying Honor at Los Angeles. Vice President Curtis late today bestowed upon

Amelia Earhart the Distinguished Flying Cross voted her by Congress for being the first woman to fly alone across the Atlantic Ocean."

The New York Times report stated: "Miss Earhart said the award is an overwhelming honor. 'I cannot but be especially grateful', she added, 'that it has been given me in Southern California where I started my flying career'." The ceremony was a part of the dedication of the State office building in Los Angeles. "Civic Square was thronged and bright with colors of the nations represented in the Olympic Games which the Vice President will open tomorrow."

Trans-Atlantic Flight to Turkey. After Costes (Chapter Two) had surpassed an RAF record of 1929 from England to Karachi, India by his 5,000 mile flight from Paris to Manchuria, two American civilians, Boardman and Polando, achieved a five thousand eleven and eight-tenths mile nonstop trans-Atlantic flight from the United States to Istanbul, Turkey. Russell Boardman and John Polando flew a Bellanca out of Floyd Bennett Field, Brooklyn, New York over July 28-30, 1931, in the time of 49 hours, for about a 12 mile increase in the world distance record. When Boardman switched off his engine, it is reported that his plane had one pint of fuel left.

The New York Times reported, Washington, July 28, (1932): "President Hoover presented the Distinguished Flying Cross to John Polando and Russell N. Boardman today for their long distance trans-Atlantic flight from New York to Istanbul, Turkey. 'I am glad', said the President, as he pinned the medals on the aviators, 'to greet you and express my appreciation and the admiration of the whole American people for your daring exploit'."

"Mr. Boardman, acting as spokesman, said in reply: 'Words fail to express the great honor which you as President of the United States have conferred upon Mr. Polando and myself in awarding to us the Distinguished Flying Cross. We acknowledge with all sincerity also our appreciation to the Senate, the House of Representatives and the War Department'."

Boardman died of injuries in 1933 when pursuing the Thompson Trophy. He was flying the treacherous Gee Bee aircraft when he crashed. A second Gee Bee crashed in the same flight, and another pilot had been killed in one earlier. Jimmy Doolittle had won the 1932 Thompson in a Gee Bee, and had walked away from a crash in another, before deciding that it was too dangerous a venture and retired from racing.

Around-the-World Flight. In 1931, flying a nearly new and customized Lockheed Vega, Wiley Post was making plans to circle the world in a whirlwind trip. He selected an Australian, Harold Gatty, former master merchant marine navigator and instructor in aero navigation, as his navigator. On June 22, they departed from New York to Newfoundland, Europe, Russia, Siberia, and Alaska to Canada, into Cleveland then New York - a total of 12 stops. Gatty and Post received DFC awards for their achievement in making an airplane trip around-the-world in eight days, fifteen hours and fifty minutes. They landed at New York City on July 1, 1931.

Post, who was enamored with aircraft as a boy, quit school and was working in the oil fields when he joined a barnstorming unit as a parachutist, earning up to $200 per jump. Working also in the oil fields to earn money for his own airplane, a chip of steel entered his left eye resulting in its loss and enough insurance money to buy a plane. He trained himself to judge distances as he engaged in a variety of flying activities until he was hired as personal pilot of F.C. Hall.

Heroism, Noted Civilians and Developments

Hall was an oilman who bought the best available aircraft which he also made available for Post for his personal use and who, encouraged his exploits. The aircraft chosen for the around-the-world flight, a Lockheed Vega, was named by Hall for his daughter, the *Winnie Mae*. In July 1933 Post repeated his around-the-world flight alone in a newer, customized Vega, and completed the trip with 11 stops in 7 days, 18 hours and 49 minutes using newly developed gyros and a radio compass.

Among other achievements in his noted career, Post developed a high altitude rubberized suit made by B.F. Goodrich. Ultimately, Post is best remembered for the Alaska crash in August 1935 which was fatal to himself and to his friend and passenger, the famous Will Rogers.

Name	Dates Award	Presented	No. Award	Medal
Amelia Earhart Putnam	07-02-32	07-29-32	56	131
Russell N. Boardman	07-11-32	07-28-32	57	134
John L. Polando	07-11-32	07-28-32	58	133
Harold Gatty	07-11-32	08-18-32	59	132
Wiley Post	07-11-32	08-18-32	60	135

Earhart's medal is engraved: "AMELIA EARHART PUTNAM", and is stamped "131".

The year closed out with three awards for flight test developments, under the provisions of WD General Orders No. 6, 1933.

Parachute Development. Master Sergeant Ralph W. Bottriel has been identified as the first Army man to risk his life in a free parachute jump from a speeding airplane. Serving in the 68th Service Squadron, Air Corps, Sergeant Bottriel performed the first ever free parachute jump in May of 1919 at McCook Field, Dayton, Ohio. At this time, parachute jumping of any kind was considered extremely hazardous. Using a manually operated parachute in the first of many jumps, he repeatedly jeopardized his life while making parachute test jumps from airplanes flying at various speeds and at various altitudes to perfect the parachute.

Sergeant Bottriel had actually made parachute jumps before testing them for the Army. In October 1918 he performed in an exhibition designed to attract attention to the Fourth Liberty Loan drive several times starting with a jump from 4,800 feet into San Antonio Air Force Base, Texas. These were made with a balloon-type parachute which opened as a result of his weight. Captain Clifford Nutt, whose DFC award was described in Chapter Two, provided the information recommending Bottriel for his citation. Bottriel was probably the 61st person awarded the DFC by the War Department.

Civilian Award by Act of Congress, March 1, 1932. Glenn H. Curtiss, who had an amazing history in aviation as a pilot, pioneer developer and manufacturer, was granted an award posthumously March 1, 1933 for his years of achievement. The New York Times, mistakenly in its report of April 10, stated: "D.S.C. FOR GLENN CURTISS - Washington, April 10 (1933) - The Distinguished Service (sic) Cross was awarded posthumously by the War Department today to Glenn H. Curtiss, the pioneer aviator who died at Buffalo on July 23, 1930. The award of the Distinguished Flying Cross was under authorization of an act of Congress on March 1, as Mr. Curtiss was not in the military service."

General B.D. Foulois, Chief Army Aviation Service, made the presentation on June 12, 1933 to Curtiss' mother, Mrs. Lula Curtiss, in Miami as noted in a New York Times article. Although considered a War Department award (Act of Congress awards have only been identified as authorized via the War Department), correspondence indicates that the Navy approved the recommendation, and just possibly may have provided the medal. Indeed, the Navy was the primary beneficiary of Curtiss' feats.

Curtiss was responsible for some of the very earliest aircraft developments, one in particular being the placement of the engine at the front of the craft rather than the rear. He led the training of pilots in the early years donating fields and time. During WWI, he developed and produced in quantity the JN series aircraft, the well-known *Jennies*, which continued on into the 20s. His medal is in the collection of the National Air and Space Museum. Since it is enclosed in a glass display case, it could not be examined by the museum specialists at my request, as to its markings.

Night-Flying Tests. Captain Donald L. Bruner, Air Corps, was honored for: "...developing and perfecting night-flying equipment in aerial flight, thus making it possible for military and commercial airplanes to traverse the length and breadth of the United States during the hours of darkness, with vision, initiative, courage, and perseverance." His award Number 63, for EXTRAORDINARY ACHIEVEMENT, was made on June 1, 1933. The medal was presented in 1933 at Patterson Field, Fairfield, Ohio.

Name	Dates		No.	
	Award	Presentation	Award	Medal
Master Sergeant Ralph W. Bottriel	tbd	01-? -33	(61)	tbd
Glenn H. Curtiss	03-01-33	06-12-33	(62)	tbd
Captain Donald L. Bruner	06-01-33	06-28-33	63	tbd

The first 63 awards, as described in the first five chapters, were mostly well recorded by the Army as to award number, sequence, and sometimes medal number. The balance of the War Department authorizations were not. In particular, ten awards in 1934 and 1935 lack this data. Seven of these awards encompass the numbers 64 through 70. However, some 10 awards were apparently made before number 71 was made in 1936. Perhaps the awards to Bronte and the two Italian officers described at the beginning of Chapter Six were not assigned numbers by the War Department. Consequently, the awards listed from this point in the book are sequenced by award number when available, or by date of approval or presentation as seems most appropriate. Award and medal numbers are only given when confirmed.

Instrument Flying - WD General Orders No. 1, 1934. Captain Albert F. Hegenberger, who was awarded the DFC for his Hawaiian flight, Chapter One, was awarded the third Oak Leaf Cluster for Extraordinary Achievement in aerial flight. "Hegenberger rendered exceptionally valuable services to the Government of the United States in the execution of a series of aerial flights culminating with a solo instrument flight and landing on May 9, 1932, in connection with the testing and development of the Air Corps System of Instrument Flying and Landing," according to his citation.

Medical Aid Flight - WD General Orders No. 8, 1934. First Lieutenant (Captain) Russell Luff Meredith, of the First Pursuit Squadron, Air Corps, was awarded the DFC for "HEROISM" in his actions on February 7, 1923. "Upon learning that an injured man was lying at the point of death on Beaver Island in Lake Michigan, (he) voluntarily made a hazardous flight from Selfridge Field to take medical aid. Extremely dangerous flying conditions were encountered, blinding snow and mists destroyed visibility, making it necessary to land on the shore to determine location. Despite discovering that his compass was in error and the supply of gasoline limited, Meredith (successfully) continued his flight due to the urgency of the mission. He thus enabled a doctor to reach the patient in time to be of service." The award was announced March 17, 1934. Major General

Dennis Nolan presented the medal to Meredith, now Captain, on April 24, 1934 at Governor's Island. A provisional battalion of the 16th Infantry was drawn up on the parade ground according, to the New York Times.

A West Point 1917 graduate, who had also served in the Field Artillery, Meredith's award was probably the 64th made by the War Department. Meredith apparently was retired due to disability in 1927, but served on active duty 1941-46. He then retired in 1948 as a Colonel and died in 1965.

California to Hawaii - Congressional Approval June 18, 1934. By Private Resolution No. 2 of the 73d Congress, the President was authorized to present the DFC to Emory B. Bronte, civilian, of San Francisco. Mr. Bronte navigated the second successful flight from California to the Hawaiian Islands under extremely adverse weather conditions in twenty-five hours, two minutes on July 14 and 15, 1927. The first flight to Hawaii by Maitland and Hegenberger was covered in Chapter One. Bronte received his medal at San Francisco on November 4, 1934 from Rear Admiral Thomas Senn. His DFC Award Certificate is said to be held at the Air and Space Museum of the Smithsonian Institute. Bronte was part of a team that included Second Lieutenant Ernest L. Smith who was awarded a DFC in March 1929 (see Chapter Three). Smith attended the presentation to Bronte according to the New York Times, November 5, 1934.

In-Flight Emergency - WD General Orders No. 3, 1935. (1 of 4 awards). For "HEROISM and EXTRAORDINARY ACHIEVEMENT", a rare dual entitlement, approved September 24, 1934, 1st Lieutenant Cornelius W. Cousland, Army Air Corps, was presented his DFC in January 1935 at France Field in the Canal Zone. The New York Times, January 3, 1935 noting the first presentation in Panama, also states: "The citation records his courage, presence of mind and complete mastery of flying."

The citation continues: "On May 31, 1934, while piloting a Douglas Amphibian near Gatun Lake at about 1,400 feet altitude, a failed portion of the right motor penetrated the pilots compartment and fatally wounded the co-pilot who fell across Lt. Cousland and the controls causing a spin. Despite his own serious injuries from flying glass, (he) ordered his passengers to retain their seats and by his courage and — complete mastery of the art of piloting maneuvered the disabled aircraft to a safe landing on — the stump-studded lake."

As Captain, Cousland was also issued a commendation for his service as co-pilot on a flight from Langley Field to Buenos Aires in February 1938 and, as Major, was awarded the Argentine decoration and diploma of Military Aviator for work in that country. After initially being held in the State Department, these were delivered to him May 30, 1942. Cousland was a West Point graduate in 1924, retired as Colonel 1949, and died in 1959.

Name	Dates		No.	
	Award	Presentation	Award	Medal
Capt. Albert F. Hegenberger	02-13-34	tbd	OLC #3	
1st Lt. Russell L. Meredith	03-17-34	04-24-34	tbd	tbd
Emory B. Bronte	06-18-34	11-04-34	tbd	tbd
1st Lt. Cornelius W. Cousland	09-24-34	01-02-35	tbd	tbd

A Balloon Exploit - July 1934. WD GO No. 3, 1935. In a joint National Geographic Society/Army Air Corps project, analogous to the Apollo program of our era, three Air Corps officers spent a long and arduous time in preparation for a technologically challenging departure from the earth, encased in a small capsule. They are shown in their flight gear in Figure 32. Their destination was neither outer space nor the moon, but was perhaps equally challenging for the existing technology. Their goal was the fringes of outer space to the earth's atmosphere at a planned altitude of 75,000 feet, some two and one-half times higher than today's commercial jets. Their project was an outgrowth of Hawthorn Gray's high-altitude flights, Chapter One, but now with an enclosed capsule instead of the open basket.

Figure 32: The three crewmen of the *Explorer I* stratospheric flight attempt. From left, Captain A. W. Stevens, Major W. E. Kepner and Lieutenant O. Anderson. *National Archives and Records Administration*

The launch site in the Black Hills, about 11 miles out of Rapid City, South Dakota, consisted of a 200-foot diameter circle - the area covered by the balloon bag. The gondola was the largest ever made so as to house the 3 crewmen and many full size scientific instruments. The world's largest free balloon, 26 stories high when inflated, required an installation of 1,500 cylinders of helium to provide the 3 million cubic feet of gas necessary to inflate the bag, seen in Figure 33. The balloon had been carefully fabricated and assembled by a team of skilled craftsmen

Wood and Canvas Heroes

Figure 33: *Explorer I* stratosphere balloon just before its takeoff on July 28, 1934 just southwest of Rapid City, South Dakota. The "26-story" tall balloon is restrained from double tethering ropes at the upper catenary band just below the dome of the balloon. They will soon be pulled off through eyelets leaving a few handropes for restraint. The large (Apollo Spacecraft-sized) spherical capsule holding three men and many scientific instruments gives a size perspective to the overall view.
Library of Congress

and women. The ground crew included 120 troopers from the 4th Cavalry.

After an exciting takeoff on July 28 and a steady ascent, the custom balloon unfortunately ruptured at 60,000 feet altitude, see Figure 34. The crew was able to partially control the descent with jettison and valve controls, however they were compelled finally to parachute to safety at about 5,000 feet. Major Kepner, being the last to jump, is said to have pushed one crewman stuck in the hatchway out with his foot. The flight ended at Holdridge, Nebraska. There is a detailed report on the project in the National Geographic magazine (see bibliography). The flight crew consisted of, Commander/Pilot - Major Kepner, Pilot/Scientific Observer - Captain Anderson, and Photographer/Scientific Observer - Captain Stevens.

Name	Dates		No.	
	Award	Presentation	Award	Medal
Major William E. Kepner	10-17-34	12-06-34	tbd	tbd
Captain Orville A. Anderson	10-17-34	12-15-34	tbd	tbd
Captain Albert W. Stevens	10-17-34	12-06-34	tbd	tbd

The DFC awards were approved in October. General A.J. Bowley presented their crosses to Kepner and Stevens as shown in Figure 35. Anderson's medal was presented nine days later at Kelly Field.

Major Kepner, who had won a Distinguished Service Cross in World War I as an Infantry Battalion Commander (Captain), 4th Infantry, knocking out German machine gun nests, became a pilot and later commanded various Pursuit Groups. Later, as Major General, he was Commanding General of the Eighth Fighter Command in Europe in World War II.

Wood and Canvas Heroes

Figure 34: The *Explorer I* which had been falling at a rate of 700 feet per minute is seen here at about 7,000 feet altitude. The fabric ripped loose can be seen hanging from the bottom of the balloon, while the canopy acts as a giant parachute. The gondola, or capsule can barely be seen, suspended on its ropes, about 100 feet below to the right.
National Archives and Records Administration

Heroism, Noted Civilians and Developments

Figure 35: Major W. E. Kepner and Captain A. W. Stevens receiving their crosses from General A. J. Bowley, December 6, 1934 at Wright Field.
National Archives and Records Administration

Anderson and Stevens were both awarded the Oak Leaf Cluster for a follow up ascent to the greatest height ever achieved to that time on November 11, 1935. Awards for the 1935 flight are described in Chapter Six.

Stevens, a photographic officer (Lieutenant) had served with the Air Service in World War I, was cited 11-22-1918 and 12-18-1918 then awarded the MSCC on May 15, 1919. He flew over the entire U.S. front line areas taking surveying photographs which were invaluable in cartographic work and strategic planning. A Purple Heart was issued in lieu of the MSCC on July 28, 1933. After the War, he was sent to McCook Field where he worked to improve aerial cameras and film.

Stevens also flew with Lieutenant Walter Hinton, U.S. Navy, in 1925 in tropical exploration flights. Hinton was noted as co-pilot of the NC-4 in Chapter One. Starting in 1923 and in later years, he conducted a project to photograph National Parks and Monuments. A heritage of his life's photos is in a collection at the National Archives. Captain Stevens was awarded the Mackay Trophy for Flight of the Year in 1929 for high altitude flights and photos. Stevens went on to further projects and honors, for which see Chapter Six.

AWARDS BY THE U.S. NAVY

Early Flight Engineering and Development Achievement Award, 1933. The only civilian to receive his award, authorized by Congress, directly from the Navy was Eugene B. Ely (award No. 19). A Curtiss flier, Ely was heavily involved in the improvement of naval aviation. In particular, he was the first ever to make a shore-to-ship flight which he accomplished January 19, 1911. Using a Curtiss pusher plane, he flew from the Presidio in San Francisco to the *USS Pennsylvania* outfitted to accept an aircraft landing, then performing a takeoff and return flight. Figure 36 shows Ely's landing. He had actually performed a takeoff two months earlier from the cruiser *USS Birmingham*. Ely's award, which was posthumous, was presented to his father, Colonel Nathan Dana Ely retired, directly by President Herbert Hoover. His citation was for "extraordinary achievement as a pioneer aviator and for significant contribution to the development of aviation in the Navy when in 1910 and 1911 he demonstrated the feasibility of operating aircraft from ships." Eugene Ely had died October 19, 1911 after an airplane crash at Macon, Georgia. The presentation ceremony at the White House is shown in Figure 37.

Figure 36: Eugene Ely landing his aircraft on the special deck of the USS *Pennsylvania* in San Francisco Bay, California, January 1911.
San Diego Aerospace Museum

Figure 37: President Herbert Hoover presents E. B. E y's posthumous award to his father, Col. N. D. Ely, retired. Others, in front, from left; Maj. Gen. Hanson E. Ely, Rear Adm. W. R. Sexton, Sec. Of War Hurley, E. L. Jahncke, Maj. Gen. G. Moseley, and Col. E. J. Ely (uncle). The scene is on the lawn of the White House, February 16, 1933.
National Archives and Records Administration

Nathan Ely appears to have served in the Navy in the Spanish American War as a seaman. He become an attorney, then entered the JAGD during WWI and retired as a Colonel. Eugene's uncles Eugene J. and Hanson E. Ely were career Army. Hanson commanded the 3rd Brigade of the 2nd Division AEF and then the 5th Division AEF. Eugene B. Ely's medal, No. 107, is said to be located at the U.S. Naval Academy, Annapolis, but cannot be found.

In-Flight Emergency, December 14, 1933. AMM2C Doyle Joseph Cavin's citation for Extraordinary Achievement read: "...as plane captain of the R-3 airplane...during an extended flight from Coco Solo, Canal Zone, to David Republic of Panama. At an altitude of 5,000 feet, the weather conditions was (sic) unfavorable. He then applied full power and started climbing at about 65 knots, still not clearing the mountain, he pulled further back on his controls, reducing speed to 40 knots and stalling the plane. It then fell into a right spin. In spite of the fact that he had been authorized by the pilot to abandon the plane...and fully realizing that the plane would most likely crash resulting in death for himself and the other passengers, Cavin remained...working calmly and intelligently manipulating the engine throttles and gasoline values. His efforts were successful; control of the plane was regained and the pilot was able to clear the mountain and veer away to safety, without the assistance of Cavin it is highly doubtful if control of the plane could have been successfully regained, thereby preventing the crash costing the lives of all its occupants."

AMM second class Cavin was presented his DFC by Rear Admiral W.S. Crosby at Fleet Air Base, Coco Solo, Canal Zone.

	Name	Dates		Medal
		Award	Presentation	No.
19.	Eugene B. Ely (Posthumous)	02-08-33	02-16-33	107
20.	AMM2C Doyle J. Cavin	tbd	07-28-34	tbd

Ely's medal is engraved:

> Eugene B. Ely for Extraordinary Achievements as a Pioneer Civilian Aviator and for His Significant Contribution to the Development of Aviation in the United States Navy
> 1910 - 1911

AWARDS TO THE UNITED STATES MARINE CORPS

<u>1931 Nicaragua Awards.</u> Only one citation is available for the activities of two men during the period of 14 to 26 July, 1931. "For Extraordinary Achievement on 22, July by Lieutenant Becker, while leading a two-plane patrol he discovered a large group of bandits in [action] on the Coto River. Despite heavy fire from the ground, during which his plane was hit twice with bullets and the accompanying plane sixteen times, he attacked the bandits with such determination and skill that their fire was silenced and many were killed. He also supported a boat landing party in the Coto River of a Guardia party...with such effectiveness that only a few stray shots were fired at the patrol by the bandits...on 26 July although weather conditions were extremely poor and it was so late in the day that after the operation he had to land his plane...after dark.... During the period from July 14 to July 22 Lieutenant Becker displayed qualities of leadership, courage, skill and determination of such high order that the aviation operations under his command and his own individual achievements in making daily patrols in extremely bad weather contributed materially to the breaking up of a large bandit concentration in North-Eastern Nicaragua and to the prevention of bandit depredations in the vicinity of Puerto Cabezas."

No citation was obtained for Sgt. Heritage, but he is listed as piloting a plane in attack against bandits in Nicaragua on July 22, 1931 and may be presumed to be the pilot of the second plane noted above.

Name	Dates Award	Presentation	Medal No.
19. 1st Lt./Col. Herbert P. Becker	03-21-32	tbd	tbd
20. Staff Sergeant Gordon W. Heritage	03-21-32	tbd	80

Becker's DFC is believed to have been presented by President Hoover. Colonel Becker had enlisted in the U.S. Army in 1918 and some four months later enlisted in the USMC as a private. He was then appointed to the U.S. Naval Academy in 1920, and commissioned in 1924. Becker was sent to various stations in the U.S. and in Cuba. He served in the Bismarck Archipelago and in China during WWII. His awards include Air Medal (for Bismark Archipelago, 2nd Nicaraguan, American Defense Base), American Campaign, Asiatic-Pacific with one star, and WWII Victory. He also was awarded the Nicaraguan Cross of Valor and the Chinese Collar, Order of the Cloud and Banner for services to China while commanding Marine Aircraft Group 25. He died August 8, 1973 (In Arlington, VA?).

The author has information that Heritage's medal was made by August Frank, and is in the hands of a private collector. The medal is engraved in straight lines, which again uses the terms "For Distinguished Service":

THE PRESIDENT OF
THE UNITED STATES
TO
STAFF SERGEANT
GORDON W. HERITAGE, USMC
FOR DISTINGUISHED SERVICE
CITATION 21 MARCH 1932

His First Flight, Emergency Rescue and Landing. Corporal Hilmer N. Torner (later Sergeant) was an operations clerk who was riding as a passenger in the rear seat of a plane piloted by Naval Aviator Staff Sergeant Orlo S. Hoffer on March 22, 1932. "At about 2 pm, while flying at approximately 2,000 feet altitude in the vicinity of Camp Kearny [San Diego], the pilot became ill and fell onto the controls of the plane in a fainting condition. The plane, entirely out of control, fell toward the ground in a spinning motion. When Torner discovered the plane was out of control, with stick and rudder locked, he stood up to jump with his parachute. But when he saw the pilot's condition and realized that by jumping it would mean death for the other man. He seized the inert body of the pilot, pulled him from the controls and succeeded in righting the plane just before it would have crashed. He was able to climb the plane to a considerable altitude and after fifteen or twenty minutes, experimenting, he was able to get the plane headed for North Island and made a very creditable landing on Rockwell Field. He then pulled the pilot out laid him out under the wing and was administering first aid when assistance arrived."

His award was announced May 27, 1932 to the papers. The New York Times headline stated: "Marine Wins Cross in First Flying on Own; Saved Fainting Pilot and Spinning Plane, for an act described as self-sacrificing heroism." The article included the statement: "Although Torner had ridden as a passenger on several flights in aircraft, he was not familiar with the controls or instruments of an airplane, and previous to this time he had never touched the controls of a plane."

The event took place on a routine flight out of NAS San Diego in airplane N2C-2, No. 8542, on a local test flight.

Name	Date Award	Presentation	Medal No.
21. Cpl. Hilmer Torner	05-27-32	06-01-32	tbd

1932 Nicaragua Awards. Two further awards for action in the second Nicaraguan campaign were made in 1932. Marine Gunnery Sergeant (pilot) Neal Williams was awarded the DFC for achievement in Nicaragua. The engraving on the reverse of the medal reads:

THE PRESIDENT OF
THE UNITED STATES
TO GUNNERY SERGEANT
NEAL WILLIAMS USMC
FOR
EXTRAORDINARY
ACHIEVEMENT IN AERIAL FLIGHTS
CITATION 20 MARCH 1933

The engraving, shown in Figure 38, is in eight lines on a later type navy, thicker and frosted planchet. Williams was cited for extraordinary achievement "as a pilot of an amphibian plane in combat with bandits in Nicaragua, and on many other occasions carrying out dangerous flying missions against bandits with determination, skill, and courage."

Heroism, Noted Civilians and Developments

Figure 38: Reverse of DFC number 116 awarded to Gunnery Sgt. N. Williams. The engraving, in typical Navy style, is reported in the text. There is no maker's mark.
Photo by J. W. Patrick, Courtesy of USMC Recruit Depot Museum, San Diego

Second Lieutenant Raymond P. Rutledge was cited for Extraordinary Achievement as a pilot attached to Aircraft Squadrons, Second Marine Brigade. He was performing an aerial search for the crew of a plane missing in the dense jungle on May 23, 1932. He found the missing crew and for the next three days made many flights 'under extremely dangerous conditions' to drop supplies and direct a ground rescue patrol. "He was engaged in this work when his plane crashed in the jungle killing him and his observer. While attached to these squadrons, Lieutenant Rutledge had flown over 400 hours in Nicaragua frequently under very adverse conditions and over difficult terrain infested with hostile bandits. An aerial attack that he conducted on May 23, 1932, against a large and dangerous force of bandits threatening Neptune Mine was credited by the Guardia Nacional de Nicaragua as decisive factor in the final dispersion of the bandit from the mine area." Thus award No. 23 for Lieutenant Rutledge became the first and only posthumous award for the Marine Corps. The 2nd Brigade Commander, General R.C. Berkeley forwarded his approval September 9, 1932.

Name	Date Award	Presentation	Medal No.
22. Sgt./Lt. Neal Williams	03-20-33	05-18-33	116
23. 2nd Lt. Raymond P. Rutledge	1932?	tbd (posthumous)	tbd

A letter from Headquarters U.S. Marine Corps indicates that the DFC and Citation for Sergeant Williams were mailed to the Commanding General, Marine Barracks, Quantico, Virginia on April 6, 1933. The medal was made available to General Lee for the formal presentation on Thursday, May 18, 1933 at Quantico, Virginia. The presentation ceremony is seen in Figure 39. The occasion for this and other Nicaraguan awards was known as Fredericksburg Day. There was a flyover of planes in formation of eight groups of three, led by Lt. Col. Ross E. Rowell.

This was followed by a dive-in formation and other aerobatics by twelve of the planes led by Lt. Lawson Sanderson, internationally known flyer, and the Marine Corps "Ace of the Air" according to the "Leatherneck" magazine of July 1933. Awards to Rowell

Heroism, Noted Civilians and Developments

and Sanderson were described in Chapter One. Williams had also been decorated on April 4, 1933 with the Nicaraguan Cross of Valor. Williams received a second DFC (not an OLC!) in WWII. At the time of his World War II award, Williams had been commissioned and was serving as a Lieutenant. Both of Williams' medals are displayed at the USMC Recruit Depot Museum at San Diego, California.

Figure 39: General Lee decorating Sgt. N. Williams May 18, 1933, Quantico, Virginia. His DFC was presented on the occasion of "Fredricksburg Day" at Quantico. *Courtesy of "Leatherneck, Magazine of the Marines"*

In October 1948 Headquarters USMC sent a letter to Mrs. Williams in Coronado, California so as "to forward to you the following posthumousmous awards: Copy of Presidential Unit Citation with ribbon bar and Star awarded the First Marine Division reinforced for service on Solomon Islands, copy of Navy

Unit Commendation with ribbon bar awarded the South Pacific Combat Air Transport Command for service in the South Pacific area, Asiatic-Pacific Campaign Medal and World War II Victory Medal." The author does not know the cause of his death.

This three year period saw awards and presentations of sixteen War Department DFCs, plus one Oak Leaf Cluster, two Navy and five Marine Corps.

CHAPTER SIX
MASS FLIGHT AND EXCITING RESCUES 1935 - 1937

GENERAL

In 1935, after a severe gust of wind caused a structural failure, the U.S. Navy rigid airship *USS Macon* crashed off Point Sur, California with two casualties. The New York Times of August 21, 1935 was full of information about the deaths of Will Rogers and Wiley Post. Included was an item about a promotion for Sergeant Stanley R. Morgan to Master Sergeant, which raised his pay from $96.60 to $144.90, (per month) for his initiative, resourcefulness, and fine judgment in finding the bodies at Point Barrow. Also, pilot Joe Crosson, an Alaskan pilot, was recommended by his congressman for a DFC for flying the bodies home - apparently never granted.

In 1936 a contract to Consolidated Aircraft Company, San Diego, was given by the Navy for the first and only four-engined flying boat, the XPB2Y, to be used in WWII. In 1937, a Seversky P-35 type Army plane won the Los Angeles to Cleveland Bendix Air Race. It continued on to set a new transcontinental record of 9 hours and 35 minutes. This aircraft later evolved into the famous World War II P-47 Thunderbolt. Also, Navy Patrol Squadron 3, with 12 PBY-1 Catalinas, flew 3,292 miles from San Diego, California to Coco Solo in the Canal Zone in just under 28 hours. United Airlines, using a DC-3, initiated Club Car service with 21 standard seats, and 14 overstuffed seats that "swivel around and can be made into a couch."

AWARDS BY THE WAR DEPARTMENT

An Italian Aerial Fleet - Public No. 31 - 74th Congress, April 10, 1935. On July 1, 1933, after intensive preparations, 25 Italian catamaran flying boats departed Rome for Chicago. A bad landing in Amsterdam cost one plane and one crew member's life, but after five other stops, 24 planes set down on Lake Michigan at Chicago, Illinois July 15 to participate in that city's World's Fair. Nevin's Time-Life book, "The Pathfinders", shows the fleet of planes at anchor in Lake Michigan. The trip was organized and conducted by Mussolini's General Italo Balbo (promoted to Air Marshall after the trip) and General Aldo Pellegrini, of the Royal Italian Air Force. On August 12, after their return flight, 23 planes set down at the mouth of the Tiber River after one more fatal crash at Lisbon and the returning airmen were greeted by Mussolini himself.

Records were not found by the author as to presentation of the DFC to Balbo, but a letter dated July 15, 1935 from the U.S. Military Attaché (in Rome?) notes the delivery of the Citation on this date, and refers to the Distinguished Flying Cross recently presented to Pellegrini. The author considers it probable that the War Department issued no award numbers for these men.

Name	Dates		No.	
	Award	Presentation	Award	Medal
Air Marshall Italo Balbo	03-10-35	06-15-35?	tbd	tbd
General Aldo Pellegrini	03-10-35	04 to 07-35?	tbd	tbd

Balbo had been active in the development of high-speed aircraft, and especially in engines suitable for winning the Schneider Trophy. In the 1920's, seaplanes were the speed champions for two main reasons: Their shorter wings suitable for long take off distances (on water), reduced in-flight drag as did their floats that were more aerodynamic than early landing gear systems. The

Italians, who had won in 1926 and lost to Britain in 1927, prepared for the 1929 Schneider by developing an 18-cylinder engine. Henry Royce, of Britain proposed sticking with a 12 cylinder but with an added supercharger. Balbo's team was disappointed losing again to the British in 1929.

Two Awards for Heroism:

In-Flight Fire - WD General Orders No. 8, 1935. For "HEROISM" on December 14, 1934, First Lieutenant Frederick L. Anderson, Jr., Air Corps, was awarded the DFC May 18, 1935. While maneuvering over San Francisco his aircraft caught fire. Directing his mechanic to jump, Anderson proceeded to jump also, until, seeing that he was directly over the city, he returned to the cockpit and although almost engulfed in flames he directed the plane away from the city then jumped into the bay where he was rescued by a crewman from the *USS Oklahoma*. The DFC was presented in July 1935 at Hamilton Field, California. His original certificate was mailed February 14, 1936, but a duplicate was issued December 21, 1942. The New York Times cites the award as being May 25, 1935, while his award card says May 18.

He graduated West Point 1928 into Cavalry then Air Corps. He served in WWII as 3rd Division Commander of the 8th Air Force, then CG Bombing Command and Deputy Chief of Operations, Strategic Air Force Europe. His awards include Distinguished Service Cross, Distinguished Service Medal, and Silver Star. He retired to disability list as Major General in 1947, and died 1969.

Passenger Rescue - WD General Orders No. 4, 1936. On June 22, 1935, Flying Cadet Francis H. McDuff, 88th Observation Squadron, Air Corps, stayed with his burning plane near Banning, California, holding it in a slow glide until two passengers had escaped. By the time Cadet McDuff was able to jump, the plane was so low he struck the ground in the first opening swing of his chute. He was uninjured. The recommendation for award for heroism was announced by General Hap Arnold on August 12, 1935 per an article in the New York Times. General Arnold recounted that the young pilot had held the flaming plane in a slow glide until Capt. Richard I. Dugan, acting as observer, and Sergeant John L. Gives had extricated themselves and made parachute leaps.

Ballooning Into Space - A Two-Man Team - WD General Orders No. 4, 1936.

Oak Leaf Clusters were awarded to two men on this GO for exploits in ballooning. After the attempt by three airmen to achieve some 70,000 feet failed, (see Chapter Five), another attempt was made by two of the same crew under the command of Captain Stevens with pilot, Captain Anderson. The expedition was again sponsored by the National Geographic Society and the Army Air Corps. On November 11, 1935, this flight was launched from the vicinity of Rapid City, South Dakota and ascended to about 72,000 feet (22,066 meters), "the greatest height ever attained by man." The balloon was successfully landed near White Lake, South Dakota.

The citation for Stevens, similar to Anderson's, for Extraordinary Achievement, read: "Captain Stevens displayed a steadfastness of purpose, a thoroughness of preparation, and professional attainments of the highest character in the execution of this flight. To his scientific knowledge may be attributed in large measure the acquisition of valuable data regarding the stratosphere." The OLCs were awarded February 6, 1936, and presented on March 7, 1936 at Kelly Field for Anderson and at Wright Field on May 12, 1936 for Stevens. Anderson, (and perhaps Stevens), at the rank of Major, later received the Prix de Henri de la Vaux award from the Federation Aeronautique Internationale for the November Mission.

Mass Flight and Exciting Rescues

Stevens, who had made a career of aerial photography since World War I, had also continued valuable cartographic surveys for the United States after WWI, had photographed national parks and monuments within the U.S. as well as western state landmarks. He arranged an expedition to Peru to take solar photographs during an eclipse, yielding useful scientific data, and eventually became director the U.S. Air Force Museum at Wright Patterson AFB. His widow donated his tremendous collection of photographs to the National Archives after his death in 1949.

Name	Dates		No.	
	Award	Presented	Award	Medal
1st Lt. Frederick L. Anderson, Jr.	05-18-36	07-03-35	tbd	tbd
Cadet Francis H. McDuff	08- -35?	tbd	tbd	tbd
Capt. Albert W. Stevens	02-06-36	05-12-36	OLC #4	
Capt. Orville A. Anderson	02-06-36	03-07-36	OLC #5	

WD General Orders No. 1, 1937, Ten Awards.

<u>Alaska Exploration, 1935.</u> Captain/Major Hez McClellan, Army Air Corps, was granted the award of the DFC posthumously on June 15, 1936 for his extraordinary achievement during the summer of 1935. He had prepared all of the plans for a flight from Washington, D.C. to Nome, Alaska, then voluntarily commanded and piloted the flight over thousands of miles of desolate country. The information secured by Captain McClellan - has proven of particular value to the Air Corps. The medal was presented to his widow, Madalyn, at Wright Field; McClellan having been killed recently while flying a new type airplane at Wright Field.

Name	Dates		No.	
	Award	Presentation	Award	Medal
Maj. Hez McClellan (Post.)	06-15-36	10-26-36	71	tbd

Flight Test Emergency, 1936. Two awards for heroism were approved October 1936 for a flight of July 22, 1936. Captains Frank G. Irvin, pilot, and John S. Griffith, co-pilot, both Air Corps, "were conducting flight tests of carbon monoxide at 2,000 feet altitude in a new airplane when the engine burst into flame. Directing a crew of observers to jump, they fought the flames by switching gas valves and using fire extinguishers, saving the plane, valuable government property, and themselves." Awards were approved October 21, 1936. Irvin's DFC was presented in December at Wright Field, Ohio, while Griffith's was presented the following February at March Field, California. Award numbers were not given, but should have been 72 and 73 respectively.

Name	Dates		No.	
	Award	Presentation	Award	Medal
Capt. Frank G. Irvin	10-21-36	12-10-36	tbd	tbd
Capt. John S. Griffith	10-21-36	02-20-37	tbd	tbd

Long Range Mass Formation Flight, 1934.
Lieutenant Colonel/Brigadier General Henry Harley (Hap) Arnold, Air Corps, was awarded the DFC for commanding a ten plane 18,000 mile flight in July and August 1934 from Washington, D.C. to Fairbanks, Alaska. Approved in 1936, the medal was presented by the Secretary of War Woodring in 1937. Arnold was Commanding General of the USAAF during World War II.

Name	Dates		No.	
	Award	Presentation	Award	Medal
Brig. Gen. Henry H. Arnold	11-25-36	01-05-37	74	tbd

In 1912, Arnold had been perhaps the first recipient of the Mackay Trophy for a flight of the year, performing a flight from College Park, Maryland, over Washington, D.C. and Fort Myer and return. Also, in June of that year he established an altitude record of 6,500 feet in a Burgess-Wright airplane as reported in the New York Times.

Arnold was a pioneer aviator. After graduating from West Point in 1907, he moved from infantry to the Air Service. He was commissioned a Major General in 1938, was Chief of the Air Force, then General of the Army (5 stars) in 1944. He is credited with building the greatest Air Force in history. His many awards include DSM + two clusters, Legion of Merit, and Air Medal. He retired, disability, 1946, was named General of the Air Force in 1949, and died in 1950. His, son H. H. Arnold Jr., graduated West Point in 1940 into Artillery, served in Anti-Aircraft, receiving a Legion of Merit and Bronze Star. He retired as Colonel in 1970 and is now deceased.

Search and Location Flight. Two officers and two enlisted men were recognized for their efforts in an aerial flight February 9, 1936. Having learned that seven Civilian Conservation Corps enrollees were stranded on an ice flow in Cape Cod Bay, (the two officers and two enlisted men), " took off in an airplane during the hours of darkness under dangerous flying conditions - located the men, dropped a message to them and reported their location, thereby being chiefly responsible for saving their lives." Awards were approved by the War Department in November 1936.

Name	Dates Award	Presentation	No. Award	Medal
Capt. Barney M. Giles	11-25-36	04-27-37	75	tbd
2nd Lt. James H. Patrick, Jr.	11-25-36	04-27-37	76	tbd
Staff Sgt. Donald E. Hamilton	11-25-36	04-27-37	77	tbd
Corp. Frank B. Connor	11-25-36	04-27-37	78	tbd

Giles was in the 20th Bombardment Squadron, Air Corps; Patrick in the Air Corps Reserve; Hamilton and Connor were of the 96th Bombardment Squadron, GHC Air Force. Awards were presented to the four men at Langley Field, Virginia.

Heroic Landing, 1935. Captain Donald W. Buckman, Air Corps, was cited for heroism while piloting a C-14 airplane carrying three passengers November 12, 1935, "(he) was seized with excruciating pain in the vicinity of his heart, when he was approximately 50 miles from his destination [Bakersfield]. Although suffering intensely, Capt. Buckman maintained control - and effected a safe landing at [the] airport, where he collapsed and died of a heart attack shortly after." Approved October 21, 1936, his posthumous medal was presented to his widow, Madeline, February, 1937 at Randolph Field, Texas.

Emergency Crash Landing. First Lieutenant Richard T. Aldworth, Air Corps, was on a flight from Mitchel Field to Langley on December 12, 1926. "While - at an altitude ...of 1,000 feet over Rockaway Beach, Long Island, the engine - instantaneously and completely failed... Lieutenant Aldworth, turning to land on the beach, saw people and a group of children and - mindful only of the safety of the crowds on the beach, ...maneuvered his airplane to avoid the crowds - and crashed into the breakers off shore. His airplane turned over immediately with great force." Although submerged and injured, Aldworth escaped and was helped ashore.

According to the New York Times, Aldworth was awarded the DFC by an executive order of President (Franklin) Roosevelt. His award, approved November 27, 1936 for Heroism ten years after the event, was presented at Mitchel Field, June 5, 1937. Major General Frank McCoy, second corps area commander, made the presentation while 800 AF Headquarters personnel were on parade and Captain Russell Scott led a multi-plane fly-over. The passage of time from the crash to recognition was attributed to the modest report Aldworth had filed, where he did

Mass Flight and Exciting Rescues

not cover his choice to crash into the ocean. Aldworth had served under Fiorello LaGuardia (later mayor of New York City), in France in the 213th Pursuit Squadron during World War I. His award card probably should have been marked No. 80. His DFC is an August C. Frank variety, and is in the hands of a private collector with other medals and ephemera.

Aldworth's medals are said to include a Silver Star, Purple Heart and Legion of Merit, as well as French and Italian medals. He was apparently a POW at the end of WWI. In WWII he recruited most of the pilots for the Flying Tigers. At the time of the presentation, Aldworth was manager of Newark Airport.

Name	Dates		No.	
	Award	Presentation	Award	Medal
Capt. Donald W. Buckman (Post)	10-21-36	02-10-37	79	tbd
1st Lt. Richard T. Aldworth	11-27-36	06-05-37	tbd	167

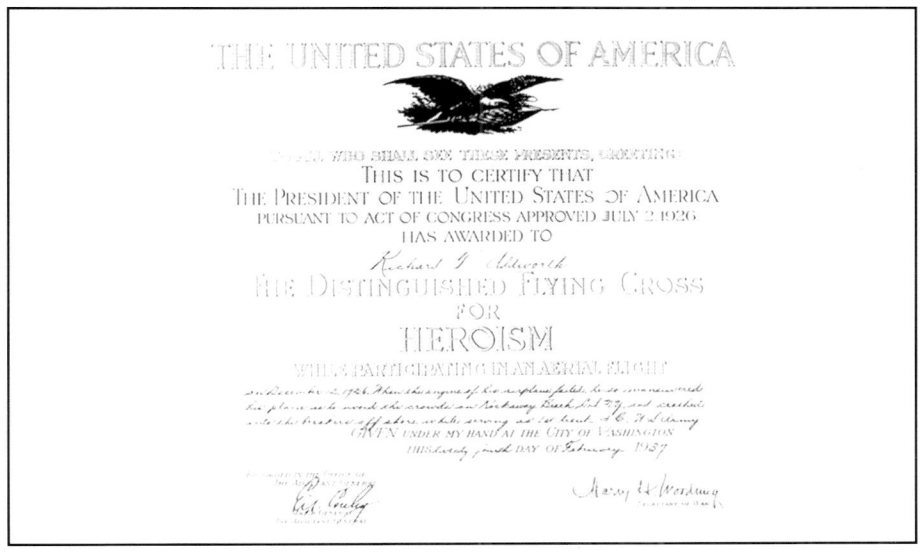

Figure 40: A DFC Certificate for First Lieutenant R. T. Aldworth, dated February 24, 1937 conveying his award for 'HEROISM'.
Courtesy of a private collector

In-Flight Emergency and Landing, WD General Orders No. 5, 1937. On November 20, 1935, Lieutenant Armstrong, Air Corps, was piloting an airplane over mountain jungles in the Canal Zone when the right engine disintegrated. With no landing spot in sight and possibility of losing the remaining engine, he ordered the three passengers and his co-pilot to bail out. The co-pilot, Lieutenant/acting Captain Wallace assisted the passengers to jump, but then returned to help the pilot. "...with courage and coolness and with the lightened airplane, they were able to effect a safe landing." The DFC was awarded to both for Heroism and Extraordinary Achievement, with Armstrong's being presented at Barksdale Field, Louisiana, and Wallace receiving his at Hamilton Field, California.

Name	Date Award	Presented	No. Award	Medal
1st Lt. James H. Wallace	05-18-37	07-17-37	81	tbd
1st Lt. Frank A. Armstrong, Jr.	05-18-37	07-10-37	82	tbd

Wallace had been cited in the Great War while a Sergeant, Transportation Corps, 21st Grand Division, Co. 92 for exceptionally meritorious and conspicuous services to A.E.F. at La Rochelle, France, awarded by General Pershing April 19, 1919.

U.S. NAVY AWARDS

Byrd Antarctic II Expedition Awards, 1936. Aviation Chief Machinist's Mate (ACMACHMATE), William Milton Bowlin and Photographer First Class (Ph1C), Joseph Arnold Pelter were approved for the DFC for services in the Antarctic. Bowlin was cited for extraordinary achievement while participating in a hazardous aerial flight of exploration (as co-pilot to the expedition) over 900 miles of crevassed areas, November 18, 1934, (Byrd Antarctic Expedition II) in the course of which a great plateau was discovered. "Bowlin showed great skill in climbing through clouds...to use the sun compass...and rare judgement...so as to prevent ice formations from causing a forced landing, his efficiency, courage, loyalty were a great credit to the Naval Service." The New York Times noted the presentation of Bowlin's DFC made by Rear Admiral W. C. Watts on March 13 (1936). Bowlin had entered the aviation service in 1918.

Pelter was cited for surveying activity in flight on November 11, 1934, while participating in a hazardous aerial flight of 1,110 miles to the southwest of Little America. A summary of his citation is engraved on the DFC as given below. Award dates are unknown, the Navy award data stating between wars 1931 to 1941. There is no manufacturer's mark on the medal.

Name	Dates		Medal
	Award	Presented	No.
21. ACMM William M. Bowlin	tbd	03-13-36	tbd
22. Ph1C Joseph A. Pelter	tbd	tbd	115

Pelter's medal, is engraved in the typical naval style and is part of the collection at the Emil Buehler Naval Aviation Library, National Museum of Naval Aviation in Pensacola, Florida.

> JOSEPH A. PELTER,
> + P.1C +
> U.S. NAVY
> FOR EXTRAORDINARY
> ACHIEVEMENT WHILE
> PARTICIPATING IN A
> HAZARDOUS AERIAL
> FLIGHT AS AERIAL
> SURVEYOR WITH THE
> BYRD ANTARCTIC
> EXPEDITION
> ON 11 NOVEMBER 1934

The cased DFC is on display at the museum.

Instrument Landing and Takeoff on Aircraft Carrier, 1935.
Lieutenant Frank L. Akers made the first blind landing on an aircraft carrier, July 30, 1935. He took off from Naval Air Station, San Diego in an OJ-2 with hooded cockpit, located the USS Langley underway in an unknown position, and landed, catching the number four wire, for which he was awarded the DFC. On May 1, 1934, Akers made a hooded landing in an OJ-2 at College Park, Maryland in the first demonstration of the system under development. In subsequent flights, Akers took off from Anacostia, and landed at College Park without assistance.[2]

23. Lt. Frank L. Akers   Award dates and Medal number tbd

Norfolk to San Francisco to Canal Zone Flight, 1935.
Acting Secretary of the Navy, Admiral William H. Standley, on behalf of President Roosevelt on April 18, 1936, presented the DFC, award No. 23, to Lieutenant Commander Knefler McGinnis. McGinnis was commander of a flight of XP3Y-1 patrol flying boats October 9, 1935 on a record setting flight from Norfolk to Cristobal Harbor Coco Solo, Canal Zone to Alameda, California. Awards were originally recommended to SecNav December 16, 1935. According to the New York Times: "McGinnis is at present under orders to report for duty on the USS Saratoga of the battle fleet." His citation was also quoted as: "This pioneering flight established a new international airline distance record of 3,443 statute miles and has materially enhanced the efficiency and military value of our naval patrol flying boats. It is an outstanding accomplishment and a great credit to Lieut. Commander McGinnis and the naval service (BuWEPS)." McGinnis is shown receiving his award in Figure 41.

Name	Dates Award	Presented	Medal No.
24. Lt.Cdr. Knefler McGinnis	04-10-36	04-13-36	tbd

Figure 41: Lieutenant Commander K. McGinnis receiving the DFC from Admiral Standley, April 13, 1936. Admiral King is to the left.
Library of Congress

U.S. MARINE CORPS AWARDS

Flight Aerobatics Development. After three years in the Ohio National Guard, Francis T. Evans was commissioned into the Marine Corps January 1909. After service in the Canal Zone and Hawaii, he was sent to Pensacola for flight training and was awarded his wings in July 1915 as Naval Aviator No. 26. When a Captain and flight instructor at NAS Pensacola, he set out to settle one of the great aeronautical controversies of the day - could a seaplane loop and spin? Many seaplanes had gone into spins and crashed causing a great loss of personnel and aircraft.

On February 13, 1917, Captain Evans, wearing no parachute, successfully looped a seaplane, an N-9 floatplane, at 3,000 feet - for the first time. After looping the plane, he succeeded in holding a steady course. The spectators below, hardly believing their eyes, gasped. The flier repeated this act to convince them. Evans then forced his plane into a spin and demonstrated recovery from spins induced by whip stalls. His citation read, in part: "These maneuvers demonstrated a greater maximum performance for seaplanes than had been thought possible and aided materially in the advancement of the science of aviation."

On February 14, 1933, a New York Times headline read: "Navy Flier May Get Cross For Confusing Mathematicians." Representative Maas of Minnesota had introduced a bill in Congress to authorize the award, with this statement: "He was my commanding officer. We had been taught in aviation schools - and it was proved mathematically - that it was impossible to take a heavy seaplane up, loop and tailspin it and live. Major Evans, without a parachute and without a desire to make a show of himself, but just to prove the mathematicians were wrong, did both these things."

The retrospective award, USMC No. 24, was authorized February 2, 1936 after action in the 74th Congress, H.R. 6576 to authorize award. Many seaplanes had previously gone into spins and crashed with great loss of life and aircraft. "The nearly universal theory was that a spin inevitably caused a fatal crash and the mathematics to prove it were taught in aviation schools. Evans took off in his N-9; with Curtiss factory representatives present, and climbed to 3,000 feet. He dove and whip-stalled repeatedly and at different speeds. The flier finally threw the airplane into a spin. As the craft fell spinning towards the earth, he pulled out of the spin, headed into the wind, and charged up to the ramp before throttling down to bring it to an easy rest on the water." Captain Evans had served as commanding officer of the

First Marine Aeronautic Company which was posted to Naval Base 13 at Ponta Delgada in the Azores in January 1918 to fly antisubmarine patrols over convoy lanes in the area. Colonel Evans retired in 1937, but was recalled to command the Marine Barracks at Norfolk in 1939. His awards include the Expeditionary Medal (12 Bronze Stars), World War I Victory (Overseas clasp for Azores), American Defense, American Campaign, and Yangtze medals.

Name	Dates		Medal No.
	Award	Presented	
24. Capt. Francis T. Evans	02-25-36	06-10-36	tbd

It is believed that Evans was presented his medal by Franklin Roosevelt.

In this chapter, sixteen War Department plus two OLCs, four U.S. Navy, and one U.S. Marine Corps awards were included.

---

[1] The wonderful photograph, not available to the author, published in the Time Life Book "The Pathfinders," David Nevin shows the fleet spread across Lake Michigan at Chicago.

[2] United States Naval Aviation 1910-60, NAVWEPS 00-80P-1, 1960.

CHAPTER SEVEN
THE PREWAR FINALE
1938 - 1941

GENERAL

The airplane and its capabilities were maturing. In 1938 Howard Hughes, in an aerodynamic design of a twin-engine Lockheed, circled the world in just over three days and 19 hours - about half of Wiley Post's five year old record, and returned to New York to a massed crowd. The year before, he had broken his previous cross-country speed record flying from Los Angeles to New York at an average of 332 miles per hour.

In the mid thirties, the Thompson and Bendix races dominated speed flying. A notable pilot Roscoe Turner was in many races and won the Thompson in 1934, as well as 1938 and 1939, the culmination of his racing career. He was also the winner of the Bendix for 1933. James Wedell had set a world speed record in 1933 and won the Thompson that year also. Two women were Bendix winners, Louise Thaden, 1936, and Jacqueline Cochran, 1938. Subsequent world records in 1938 and 1939 fell to German military aircraft as World War II neared.

Among other news, the New York Times reported on September 25, 1938; "The tragic death of Major Gen. Oscar Westover, chief of the Army Air Corps, in a plane crash at Burbank, California last Wednesday was a great loss for civil as well as military aviation". He was succeeded by "Hap" Arnold. It also reported on the same date, that the Twentieth Pursuit Group had been assigned one P-36 aircraft whereupon their old P-26 Boeings had been transferred out leaving them with one aircraft for 53 pilots!

Following direction of the President, the Navy established a Neutrality Patrol of air and ship reconnaissance of sea approaches to the United States, in September 1939.

Captain John H. Towers, commanding the USS Saratoga was made assistant chief of the Bureau of Aeronautics for the second time. He exchanged places with Captain Albert C. Read. Towers, the most senior naval pilot and an aviator since 1911, had commanded the 1919 trans-Atlantic flight and piloted the NC-3, unsuccessfully, while Read had piloted the successful NC-4.

As a footnote to this period with respect to Naval aviation, the USS Langley, the first United States Aircraft Carrier was sunk by enemy air attack, February 27, 1942, 74 miles off her destination of Tjiulatjap, Java, while ferrying 32 Army P-40 s. The Langley had been the site of naval carrier development from 1922 to 1936 when it was recommissioned as a seaplane tender.

AWARDS BY THE US WAR DEPARTMENT

WD General Orders No. 1, 1938, Three Heroism Awards. Also, Extended Flight, all Published in Supplement II, American Decorations, July 1, 1937 - June 30, 1938, (ref. Al Gleim).

Pilot Blown Out of Cockpit. One of the more unusual incidents in early aviation occurred April 24, 1937 on a flight from Hensley Field, Texas to Oklahoma. "About 40 miles out of Hensley at 4,000 feet altitude, the pilot's parachute was inadvertently released, pulling him out of the plane where his body broke off the left tail and damaged the rudder. The passenger, Lieutenant Ellis, Air Reserves, U.S. Army, believing the pilot to be badly injured, took over control of the plane so as to more quickly report the accident. He successfully returned to Hensley and landed the badly damaged airplane and then served as observer in another plane returning to the location of the accident and finding the body of the pilot who had been killed." Second Lieutenant Dross Ellis was presented his medal at Randolph Field, Texas.

The citation was "For Heroism - in aerial flight from Hensley Field, Texas to Oklahoma - Lieutenant Ellis, a passenger, disregarding his own safety, and having in mind securing assistance for the pilot, whom he believed to have been seriously injured, piloted the badly damaged airplane back to Hensley Field and, at the risk of his life, landing it safely."

<u>Engine Failure and Fire.</u> First Lieutenant Benjamin S. Kelsey, Army Air Corps, was cited for Heroism and Extraordinary Achievement for landing at Wright Field, December 24, 1936 after his left motor failed and the left wing burst into flames. "On a flight from Mitchel Field, and in darkness at risk of his life he prevented the destruction of valuable government property by making a safe landing." In a later quote in the New York Times, Lieutenant Kelsey stated "that he stuck with his plane to save a toy train on the Christmas Eve, a present for his small son, when flames attacked one wing of his plane and he made a dash to Wright Field." Brigadier General Augustine W. Robbins presented him his medal in March 1938 at Wright Field, Ohio.

Kelsey was also known for having flown the front seat in a training plane, September 24, 1929, piloted by then Lieutenant James H. Doolittle. The flight was noteworthy in that Doolittle was completely enclosed in a canvas hood. Flying by radio and instruments only, he took off, climbed to 1,000 feet, banked 180 degrees flying back over Mitchel Field, he again turned and touched down and landed in the first public demonstration of blind flying. Kelsey, acting as a safety backup, did not once touch the controls as he signaled during the landing by holding his hands above his head.

In a further moment in history, on February 11, 1939, Lieutenant Kelsey was pulled from the crash of a secret pursuit plane that had been engaged in secret speed trials across country, apparently averaging between 350 and 400 miles per hour. Colonel Kelsey was awarded the DSM for his work as Project Officer of AF production development, especially the P-38, from 1940 to 1943. Kelsey attained the rank of Brigadier General, and retired December 31, 1955.

In-Flight Failure. Homer A. Boushey, Jr., Army Air Corps, also was cited for Heroism and Extraordinary Achievement for aerial flight on October 5, 1936; "While descending from an altitude performance flight in a new type airplane, a structural failure...resulted in the loss of both ailerons...after a descent of about 2,000 feet, the pilot, second Lieutenant Boushey motioned to his mechanic to jump, then by skillful use of the remaining controls and at the risk of his life, brought the airplane to a safe landing and made possible an engineering study of the structural failure." Lt. Boushey's DFC was presented to him April 1938 at Fort Lewis, Washington.

Name	Dates		No.	
	Award	Presentation	Award	Medal
2nd Lt. Dross Ellis	12-21-37	02-12-38	83	tbd
1st Lt. Benjamin S. Kelsey	02-03-38	03-09-38	84	tbd
2nd Lt. Homer A. Boushey, Jr.	02-03-38	04-06-38	85	tbd

Argentina Flight of February 1938. For planning and commanding an extremely hazardous and exacting flight of six flying

The Prewar Finale

fortress B-17 airplanes from Langley Field to Buenos Aires, Lt. Colonel Robert Olds, Army Air Corps, was recommended for the DFC April 1, 1938. The flight covered a thirteen-day period from February 15 to 27th. The citation states Olds was responsible for planning and execution of this flight in the interest of Pan-American amity. His DFC was presented to him at Langley Field, Virginia, April 1938 per award No. 86. Figure 42 shows Olds receiving his medal from Major General Frank M. Andrews.

Figure 42: Gen. F.M. Andrews pins DFC on Col. R. Olds for South American mercy flight. The award was presented at Langley Field, Virginia, April 30, 1938.
Library of Congress

Just 7 days previous to the presentation, Olds had set two cross-country records in flights from Langley, Virginia to Riverside, California and back. He covered the 2,285 mile trip in 12 hours, 27 minutes, one hour less than previous military aircraft records.

Wood and Canvas Heroes

His return to Langley setting down at 4:00 am, April 23, 1938 took 10 hours, 45 minutes - 16 minutes under the previous record for military aircraft, according to the New York Times.

On December 19, 1941 Colonel Olds was given a commendation by the Air Corps for his services in participating in aerial flight to Rio de Janeiro, and he had previously been awarded the Order of the Southern Cross, rank of Officer, by the President of Brazil for his participation in celebrations in Rio de Janeiro for the 50th anniversary of Brazil after a November 11 to 25, 1939 flight from Langley. Major Gen. Olds was awarded the DSM as Commanding Officer of the Ferrying Command, having pioneered the Ferry Service from Canada to England.

Name	Dates		No.	
	Award	Presentation	Award	Medal
Col. Robert Olds	04-12-38	04-30-38	86	tbd

WD General Orders No. 5, 1939, Supplement III, American Decorations, July 1, 1938 - June 30, 1939, Two Awards.

<u>Mercy Flights, Langley AFB to Chile.</u> Captain/Major Caleb V. Haynes, AAC, for extraordinary achievement while participating in aerial flight from Langley Field, Virginia to Santiago, Chile, Feb. 4, 5 and 6, 1939. "As commander and pilot of the XB-15, [he] transported without hesitation and under emergency orders, a total of three thousand two hundred and fifty pounds of Red Cross medicinal supplies to Santiago, Chile under conditions which were extremely hazardous and exacting. Loaded to absolute maximum capacity, the XB-15, under the superior pilotage of Major Haynes, cleared Langley Field before daylight - and adhered to a rigid flight schedule which involved the penetration of unfavorable flying weather, a night landing at Panama, night takeoffs at Panama and Lima - and an arrival on schedule at Santiago early February 6, 1939." The award was made for his Flight of Mercy of 4,933 miles.

The Secretary of War Harry H. Woodring presented his medal at The State Department, February 1939. Figure 43 shows the pinning of his DFC. Mr. and Mrs. Caleb H. Haynes were present at the ceremony. The New York Times reported a fifty-plane flyover, but it may not have been included considering that the presentation was in the State Department.

Figure 43: Secretary of War H.A. Woodring presenting the DFC to Major C.V. Haynes, February 14, 1939 at the State Building, Washington, DC. At the right, Senor Don Sergio Huneeus, Charge d'Affaires Embassy of Chile, in recognition of Haynes mercy flight to Chile.
Library of Congress

This was not the first citation or award to Haynes, nor would it be his last. He became the only person in this period to receive a total of three DFC awards as well as others.

Major Haynes was given a letter of Commendation in February 1938 as a pilot for his flight from Langley to Buenos Aires. Again he received a letter of Commendation for a flight in August 1938 to the Republic of Columbia as commander of B-17 #80, from Langley to Bogota, for the inauguration ceremonies of the President, Dr. Eduardo Santos. This was followed by the DFC in February 1939 and the award of the Al Merito by Chile 9-2-39. He was susequently authorized by Congress to accept the awarded message and souvenir, decoration and Diploma.

As Lieutenant Colonel and Chief of the North Atlantic Division of the Air Corps Ferrying Command, he was awarded Oak Leaf Cluster No. 6 to the DFC for commanding and piloting a flight from Bolling Field to Prestwick, Scotland, July 1941 under wartime conditions in an unarmed aircraft, per WD GO No. 5, 1942. The flight lasted 28 hours in strict wartime conditions including barrage balloons and blackout. The OLC was presented March 28, 1942 at Borinquen Field, Puerto Rico.

Again, from August 31 to October 7, 1941 he commanded and piloted a B-24 flight from Bolling AFB over the South Atlantic to Basra, Iraq. This round trip flight was over 26,000 miles with a total elapsed flying time of 109 hours at an average speed of 238 mph and with stops at 14 strange airports, which were in general too small for an aircraft the size of the B-24. He was awarded his second OLC, the eighth OLC awarded, per WD GO No. 19, 1942. It was presented April 5, 1943 at New Delhi, India. Haynes was the only three-time winner of the DFC for actions before, or early, World War II, not considering possible early combat awards. He became a Brigadier General in WWII, and at some point was awarded the Silver Star, citation unknown.

The Prewar Finale

Name	Dates		No.	
	Award	Presentation	Award	Medal
Capt. Caleb V. Haynes	02-09-39	02-14-39	87	tbd
Oak Leaf Clusters	12-17-41	03-28-42	OLC #6	
	02-14-42	04-05-43	OLC #8	

Canal Zone to Chile. Captain Franklin C. Wolfe, Army Air Corps, was flight commander and chief pilot on one of two planes assigned to relief flights from Panama. "Taking off from the Canal Zone on - short notice - carrying medical and other supplies to the earthquake-stricken area of Chile, Captain Wolfe flew more than 3,400 miles over an unfamiliar route. Immediately after arrival and for the next 10 days, Captain Wolfe and the other members of the flight - flew day and night - in territory over which they had never before flown and transported in all about 10,000 pounds of medical supplies, food and mail - at the same time evacuating to safety some 65 persons." The flights were performed in the period of January 28 through February 13, 1939.

Name	Dates		No.	
	Award	Presentation	Award	Medal
Capt. Franklin C. Wolfe	tbd	07-07-39	tbd	tbd

Major General Stone is shown decorating Captain Wolfe at France Field, Canal Zone in Figure 44.

Supplement IV, American Decorations, July 1, 1939 - June 30, 1940, Eight Awards.

Development and Test, High-Altitude Flight. Major Carl F. Greene and Captain Alfred H. Johnson, Army Air Corps, "...despite a history of failures and fatalities in high-altitude pressure cabin operations, at great personal risk, chose to continue the research. For a period of two years they conducted tests

Wood and Canvas Heroes

Figure 44: Maj. Gen. Stone presents DFC to Captain F.C. Wolfe for his flight to Chile. The presentation, July 7, 1939, was made at France Field, Canal Zone, Panama. *National Archives and Records Administration*

and served in the first successful flight tests. With Captain Johnson as pilot and Major Greene as technical observer and cabin pressure operator they became the first to demonstrate practical high-level airplane operation to the Distinction of the United States Army Air Corps."

Alfred Henry Johnson was West Point class of 1926. He served in WWII in the FEAF (Far Eastern Air Forces) as a Brigadier General, and received the DSM. He retired in 1957 as Major General.

Automatic Landing System. During the years of 1935 through 1937 Captains George V. Holloman and Carl J. Crane, Army Air Corps, designed, developed, and flight tested an airplane automatic landing system that by August 1937 made possible the first complete automatic airplane landing in history. Hundreds of flights were conducted with complete disregard for their own personal safety. Award No. 91, for Extraordinary Achievement, approved July 10, 1939 was made to Holloman, who, (no award card was located for Crane) was presented his medal July 1939. According to this citation, "Captain Holloman with utter disregard of his personal safety, performed virtually all of the great amount of flight testing which was required for the numerous items of equipment which go to make up the complete automatic landing system, and, when finally on August 23, 1937, the first experimental automatic landing flights were made, he was in the cockpit of the airplane." Captain Crane's citation and dates are likely to be the same.

In-Flight Refueling. First Lieutenants Virgil Hine, Army Air Service and Frank W. Seifert, Army Air Service, were awarded the DFC by Act of Congress April 30, 1940 for their early work on in-flight refueling. With Hine as pilot and Seifert manipulating the hose lines, the two men made repeated contact with an endurance aircraft supplying gasoline, oil, and water for an endurance record. Their feat was performed June 28-29, 1923 in support of Lieutenants L. Smith and J. Richter whose 1929 DFC awards were noted in Chapter Three.

Name	Dates		No.	
	Award	Presentation	Award	Medal
Maj. Carl F. Greene	tbd	tbd	tbd	tbd
Capt. Alfred H. Johnson	tbd	tbd	tbd	tbd
Capt. George V. Holloman	07-10-39	07-15-39	91	tbd
Capt. Carl J. Crane	tbd	tbd	tbd	tbd
1st Lt. Frank W. Seifert	04-30-40	tbd	tbd	tbd
1st Lt. Virgil Hine (Posthumous)	04-30-40	tbd	tbd	tbd

Air Force installations were named for two of the men above, Seifert Field, Chicago, Illinois, and Holloman Air Force Base, Arizona.

Supplement V, American Decorations, July 1, 1940 - June 30, 1941, Seven Awards.

Flight Testing Award. Over a period of $4^{1}/_{2}$ years, Captain Samuel R. Harris Jr., Army Air Corps, "flight-tested more than 200 different types of airplanes, many of extremely hazardous, experimental design without the loss of a single airplane. Despite frequent forced landings due to experimental engine or structural failures, Captain Harris courageously continued to flight-test - in the most strenuous maneuvers possible to ascertain their safety, efficiency, and suitability for air combat." His award, No. 95 was issued in July 1940, and resulted in presentation of his medal at Wright Field, Ohio.

Samuel Russ Harris, Jr. was a West Point graduate 1926. He served at Hq. AAF in 1941-44, receiving the DSM. In 1944-45 he commanded the 499th Bomb Group, 20th AF in the Southwest Pacific, Philippines. His awards include the Bronze Star. He retired in 1956 as Major General, and died 1969.

In-Flight Engine Failure. First Lieutenant Harold L. Neely, Army Air Corps, was awarded the DFC for Heroism when, "while flying at 11,000 feet over Kansas, December 18, 1939 in a severe dust storm, he lost both engines of a large Army airplane. Signaling to three passengers to jump, he observed two of them exit the plane, but believed the third man to be still aboard. Not willing to jump with the third man still aboard, and disregarding his personal safety, he brought the craft down flying blindly through the storm, and safely crash landed. He then discovered that all three passengers had made a safe exit."

The Prewar Finale

High-Altitude Flight Testing. Private Raymond U. Whitney, Army Medical Department, eighth enlisted man to be awarded a DFC and the only private (PFC) was a U.S. Medical Department Laboratory Technician. His award, No. 97, approved July 1940, was for heroism in aerial flights. "For more than two years, Whitney voluntarily permitted himself to be subjected to experiments of effects of high altitudes and great pressures to determine the effects on the human body. Despite a history of failures and fatalities, this included participating in test flights of an experimental substratosphere cabin where failure would be fatal." Presentation was made to Pfc. Whitney, September 1940 at Wright Field.

Landing Gear Failure Award. While Captain George E. Price, Army Air Corps pilot, was performing a high-speed power calibration test on January 6, 1940 in a new type of aircraft, "...a structural failure caused the landing gear to be locked in a partially retracted position. Disregarding his personal safety, and despite a loss of his radio transmitter, Captain Price signaled his intentions to land and received a one-way radio message to land alongside the runway in snow. He successfully accomplished a landing without material damage, thereby saving the benefit of two years intensive research on the airplane."

In-Flight Engine Failure. The DFC was awarded to Second Lieutenant/Captain Willard W. Lazarus, and Sergeant Thomas F. O'Malley, both Army Air Corps, in December 1940 "...for their coolness and courage on a flight from Puerto Rico to the Virgin Islands on March 5, 1940. At 2,500 feet both engines stopped. Lt. Lazarus ordered 4 non-flight officers and his crew chief, O'Malley, to bail out while maneuvering the plane to assist their jumping. Instead of jumping himself, Sgt. O'Malley assisted the four officers, inexperienced in flying, in vacating the plane, undoubtedly contributing to their safe descent, then turned to help the pilot, rendering valuable assistance in the safe landing of the airplane. By great coolness and skill (the pilot) maneuvered the plane to permit the four passengers to jump, then landed so skillfully that the airplane was not damaged."

Awards were announced January 8, and the crosses were presented at Borinquen Field, Philippine Republic on January 17, 1941. Private Thomas F. O'Malley, then of the 2nd Sanitary Troop, had been cited June 25, 1919 for gallantry in action against the enemy in the St. Mihiel Sector in France by the Second Division.

Control Stick Failure. First Lieutenant William T. Hudnell, Jr., Army Air Corps, awarded the DFC for heroism, was making an aerobatic flight at 2,000 feet in a P-36A April 23, 1940 at Langley Field, Virginia. While descending, his control stick locked in the neutral position. Convinced that his aircraft could damage property and injure residents if he bailed out, he fought to land the plane. His first attempt was unsuccessful, but rather than risk the damage that his plane might cause, he tried again and succeeded in a safe landing.

The presentation of his DFC was scheduled for January 1941, but had to be postponed. On February 8 General Arnold visited the field and conducted an inspection preventing the rescheduled ceremony. Then, because of weather, there was another postponement. In the meantime, Lt. Hudnell's wife fell on the ice, broke her leg and wound up in the Mitchel Field Hospital. Rescheduled to February 15, at 9:00 am everything was prepared for (the now) Captain Hudnell. The 3,500 men for a parade were formed into units, 350 officers were in place, and 54 of the latest camouflaged P-40 airplanes were on the line, 2 news reel men were setting up, and the base meteorologist predicted sunshine in 1/2-hour. Suddenly the ceremony was called

The Prewar Finale

off. The base doctor, after checking Hudnell who was not feeling well, announced that he had measles and would be quarantined for 15 days.

One officer was quoted as stating that the next date selected should be kept a military secret. After one more delay due to weather, Hudnell was finally pinned by Brigadier General John B. McDonnell on March 7, 1941.

Name	Dates Award	Presentation	No. Award	Medal
Capt. Samuel R. Harris, Jr.	07-31-40	09-24-40	95	tbd
1st Lt. Harold L. Neely	tbd	tbd	tbd	tbd
Pvt. Raymond U. Whitney	07-31-40	09-24-40	97	tbd
Capt. George E. Price	tbd	tbd	tbd	tbd
2nd Lt. Willard W. Lazarus	12-23-40	01-17-41	99	tbd
Sgt. Thomas F. O'Malley	12-23-40	01-17-41	100	tbd
1st Lt. William T. Hudnell, Jr.	tbd	03-07-41	tbd	207

Hudnell's DFC reverse and edge-impressed number are shown in Figure 45. His medal is held by a private collector.

Figure 45: Reverse of DFC for W.T. Hudnell, shown in two views, the reverse view with his name, and the edge view with number 207. No maker's name appears on the medal. *Photos courtesy of an anonymous collector.*

Final Pre-World War II Events - September to November 1941. Two commanders, Colonel Eugene L. Eubeck and Major Emmett (Rosie) O'Donnell, Jr. led successive formations of B-17s from San Francisco to the Philippine Islands over 10,000 miles of uncharted courses starting in September 1941. They, and perhaps as many as 75 officers and men of their command were recommended December 25, 1941 for the DFC for their achievements. O'Donnell (West Point 1928) became a Brigadier General commanding a Bomb squadron, then a Wing in the 20th AF. He was eventually CinC of the Pacific AF 1959-63 and retired in 1963 as a General. They are not included in further detail in this book since their award did not occur until after the start of the war, and because Howard Mingo covers the episode in his "American Heroes of the War in the Air" including the description of their ordeal and names as well as photos.

Mingo does not cover medal numbering data, but at least one crew member is known to have received medal No. 561. According to an anonymous collector, this medal, edge numbered and named, was awarded to Erwin J. Dobberpfhul, hand-engraved and is accompanied by a 1926 style certificate. Sergeant Dobberpfhul was listed in Mingo for the DFC. The New York Times also provides listings of crewmembers, their rank, age, and city of enlistment in the issue of December 22, 1941.

Summary of Early Oak Leaf Cluster Awards (OLC)
After 1927 by the WD

1. Ira C. Eaker	G.O. 7, 1929	Presented Mar. 02, 1929
2. James Doolittle	G.O. 16, 1929	Presented Oct. 25, 1929
3. Albert F. Hegenberger	G.O. 1, 1934	Presented tbd.
4. Orville A. Anderson	G.O. 4, 1935	Presented Mar. 07, 1936
5. Albert W. Stevens	G.O. 4, 1935	Presented May 12, 1936
6. Caleb V. Haynes	G.O. 5, 1942	Presented Mar. 28, 1942
7. tbd		
8. Caleb V. Haynes	G.O.19, 1942	Presented Apr. 05, 1943

U.S. NAVY AWARDS

Seaplane Crash, Heroic Crew Rescue Activities, 1938.
Heroism awards were recommended for two ACMMs on April 1, 1939 for their heroic conduct following the collision of two USN PBY-2 Seaplanes during fleet exercises on February 2, 1938. One plane was badly damaged and crash-landed, but filled rapidly with water and was near sinking. ACCM Vernon O. Hatfield, stunned with a broken knee and other contusions, went immediately to the aid of other crew, rescuing one from drowning, and attempting to rescue another man, unsuccessfully. Donald B. McKay, with a broken leg and hand, dove underwater inside the aircraft to retrieve a life raft thereby preventing greater loss of life.

25. ACMM Vernon Owen Hatfield, Dates and Medal number tbd
26. ACMM Donald Bernard McKay, same

Emergency Landing by Non-Pilot, 1938. "...on September 22, 1938, Radioman Second Class [Otto Phelps was] a passenger in an SBC-3 airplane...during dive-bombing practice, on Upper Thoro Island, New Jersey. When the plane was making the third dive, the pilot was accidentally thrown from it, leaving Phelps in the rear seat with the plane in a near vertical dive. He pulled the plane out of the dive and brought it under his control. Although not a qualified pilot, and without the aid of wheels, stabilizer, and propeller pitch control, he successfully landed the plane on the field...with only minor damage." The feat occurred at Cape May.

27. RM2C Otto Russell Phelps, award announced April 1, 1939 by Secretary Swanson, medal number tbd.

Phelps received a Gold Star as a second DFC award in the early days of WWII as a Chief Radioman, citation not seen.

For Heroism in In-Flight Emergency, 1939. While piloting an SB2U-1 on August 31, 1939 "...at an altitude of three thousand feet, Ensign Eoff's plane experienced a complete engine failure. Since the terrain was not suitable to attempt a landing, he gave his radioman a chance to jump but the latter's parachute fouled the structure of the airplane and he dangled beneath the fuselage. Attempts to shake him off failed, and the extra weight and drag of the man suspended - caused [the plane] to stall and crash to the earth with terrific force, killing [Eoff] and his passenger."

28. Ensign James H. Eoff, Posthumous award, dates and medal number tbd.

Two Awards for 1939-40 Antarctic Flights. For participating in hazardous flight in the antarctic, pilot Ashley Snow and Radioman Earle Baker Perce, were awarded the DFC. Their "...flights were made exploring over 700 miles of coastline over broken ice where a forced landing would result in a crash and where rescue would be practically impossible. Particularly outstanding was the final evacuation of the personnel from the East Base on March 22, 1941."

Lt. jg Ashley Clinton Snow, Jr. was awarded the DFC at the time of the Battle of Midway, citation not seen.

29. CRa Earle Baker Perce, dates and Medal No. unknown
30. ACMM Ashley Clinton Snow, dates and Medal No. unknown

Extraordinary Heroism in In-Flight Rescue, 1941. On May 15, 1941, Lieutenant Walter S. Osipoff, USMC, was performing a training parachute jump from an R2D-1 airplane over San Diego NAS, when the shrouds of his partly opened parachute became entangled with the static cord and other rip cords, head down, he dangled helplessly about one hundred feet below and astern of the plane. "Two Navy test pilots on the ground observed this, and on their own initiative, took off in an SOC-1 aircraft to attempt a rescue. Lieutenant Lowrey [who was at the controls], skillfully maneuvered his plane until after several attempts, [ACMM] McCants standing in the rear cockpit, was able to grasp Lieutenant Osipoff, and insert part of his body, head first, into the rear cockpit."

"While McCants was attempting to cut the [parachute] shrouds, ...bumpy air threw the propeller of the SOC plane into the tail fairing of the Douglas, cutting off about 12 inches of the fairing cone as well as the entangled shrouds. [Now, with Lowrey's] plane encumbered with shroud and a part of the parachute itself fouling the empennage, and the additional weight of an extra passenger, partly out of the rear cockpit, Lieutenant Lowrey skillfully maneuvered his plane to a safe landing."

The two rescuers were recommended for the DFC May 27, 1941. Crosses were presented at Coronado Naval Air Station, California to:

Name	Dates		Award No.
	Award	Presented	
31. Lt. William W. Lowrey	tbd	06-05-41	tbd
32. ACMM John R. McCants	tbd	06-05-41	tbd

The New York Times stated that the crosses were presented by Secretary Know who was quoted as conveying President Roosevelt's congratulations on "one of the most brilliant and daring rescues within the annals of our naval history."

Twenty-Two Year Award for Heroic Dirigible Action of 1925.
This DFC award could be considered as Pre-World War II or post-World War II, but is arbitrarily listed here as award No. 33

despite the numerous wartime awards that would have preceded it. By Act of Congress June 30, 1947, the Navy was directed to award the DFC to Rear Admiral Charles E. Rosendahl, "in recognition of his heroic action as commanding officer of the Navy Dirigible United States Ship *Shenandoah* on September 3, 1925, on the occasion of its destruction and loss during a violent storm, - particularly for the - successful navigation of the airborne remnant of the airship without injury to the survivors of the catastrophe."

A description of the event in NAVWEPS 00-80-P (B) states that the rigid airship was torn apart in a line squall before daylight over Ohio. This account states that "...the control car and after section fell directly to the ground, while the forward section free-ballooned for an hour, saving all hands when it landed about 12 miles away." The report also says that, "Lieutenant Commander Zachary Lansdowne, commanding officer, was killed, with fourteen others." In all, there were 29 survivors.

On August 5, 1929, Rosendahl boarded the German *Graf Zeppelin* at Lakehurst, New Jersey on its great trans-Atlantic flight to Friedrichshafen, Germany, and its return to Lakehurst via Russia, Siberia, Japan, the Pacific Ocean, and continental United States. The dirigible was 700 feet in length with a 100-foot long gondola. As a Lieutenant Commander, Rosendahl was later captain of the *Los Angeles* lighter-than-air craft. In October of 1931 he became Commanding Officer of the rigid airship *Akron* (ZRS-4). The following month the *Akron* carried 207 individuals aloft, a new record for a single craft.

33. Charles L. Rosendahl award 6-30-47 (retrospective) medal number tbd.

The Prewar Finale

U.S. MARINE CORPS AWARDS

Aerial Search and Rescue Award, March 1939. (Act of Congress 2-25-36). A 1922 Naval Academy graduate, Clayton C. Jerome first drew attention to his flying in January 1930, when, practicing acrobatics over San Diego at 2,000 feet, the hand control stick of his plane broke off. Rather than bail out and risk death and damage to the population, he stayed with the plane. "He righted the craft to normal flying position by maneuvering the socket with his hand; then lashing the stick back to the socket with his handkerchief, trouser belt, and necktie, with which he made a successful landing." While this might seem to warrant a DFC, this award was actually made for his activiies in April 1937.

"On April 23, 1937, an airplane of the Venezuelan Government, ...crashed in the dense jungles of the Cuyuni, as a result of which two of [nine] occupants were killed...Captain Jerome, then serving as Naval Attaché...reported promptly from Panama in response to the request for aid of the American minister to Venezuela, and for ten days made almost daily flights over extremely hazardous and unexplored mountain and jungle terrain.... When the survivors were finally located,...he showed rare flying skill and courage in twice landing [with his amphibian plane] in the narrow jungle river, with protruding rocks and overhanging trees, and in bringing out to safety four occupants of the ill-fated plane, one of whom was most seriously injured. The take-off from the very narrow river, having numerous obstacles, was most hazardous. His conduct, foresight, courage and flying skill on this occasion were distinguished and outstanding."

Name	Dates Award	Presented	Award No.
25. Capt. Clayton C. Jerome	08-29-38?	03-24-39	tbd

This was the last USMC award prior to World War II. Jerome was a 1922 graduate of the U.S. Navy Academy. Before WWII he served in China and Nicaragua, and, as Naval Attaché for Air, to eight different Central or South American governments. He was serving in the later capacity when he won his DFC.

Lieutenant General Jerome (retired rank) served in five campaigns in WWII and in Korea where he commanded the First Marine Aircraft Wing and for which he received the Distinguished Service Medal and his fourth Legion of Merit (both from the Army Air Force). Two prior Legion of Merit awards were for the Northern Solomons, Treasury-Bouganville, Bismarck, Archipelago and Luzon and Mindanao. The first award was with combat "V". His third award was from the Air Force for service at Luzon in the Philippines. He died February 15, 1978. Postwar he commanded MCAS Quantico then served in various Headquarters assignments, and eventually was Commanding General, Aircraft, Fleet Marine Force, Pacific at El Toro Marine Air Corps Station, California.

U.S. COAST GUARD AWARDS

The Coast Guard awards were not authorized in the original Act of Congress. The Coast Guard was not recognized for award of the DFC until 1937. At this time, the Coast Guard was part of the Department of The Treasury. The author's limited research has not discovered any data as to medals source nor numbering assignments. Awards of the DFC to the Coast Guard continue to this day.

Sea Emergency Flight, June 1935. Lieutenant C. B. Olson was cited as the first Coast Guard aviator to receive the DFC, in recognition of a 1935 flight of 300 miles from Miami to an Army Transport ship at sea, in storm and darkness. His citation read;

The Prewar Finale

"For transportation of a seriously ill army officer from the Transport *Republic* the lieutenant having shown extraordinary skill and courage, - landing without mishap, alongside the transport in rough sea." Award No. 1 was presented to Olson by Secretary of the Treasury Morganthau on May 12, 1938.

Mercy Mission 1937. The DFC was approved for Lieutenant Commander Frank Ashton Leahy, commandant of the U.S. Coast Guard Base at Salem, Massachusetts September 9, 1938. Using radio direction finding equipment to locate a trawler, he had picked up and carried "an injured seaman from Georges Banks by air to the mainland under adverse conditions on May 21, 1937. The officer flew to the banks in a Coast Guard flying ambulance at night and landed in heavy seas to take Chief Engineer Edward R. Johnson from the Boston trawler *Whitecap*." Johnson's left arm had been severed by an ice-making machine.

	Name	Dates		Medal
		Award	Presentation	No.
1.	Lt. C. B. Olson	tbd	05-12-38	tbd
2.	Lt.Cdr. Frank Ashton Leahy	11-09-38	tbd	tbd

Although previous awards lists have ended at June of 1941, the National Archives has advised the author that no DFCs were awarded from July through December 7, 1941. This chapter closes listing nineteen War Department, nine U.S. Navy, one U.S. Marine Corps, and two U.S. Coast Guard Awards.

Appendix I

EARLY PILOTS
SIGNAL CORPS MILITARY AVIATION BADGE QUALIFIED PILOTS

By date of qualifying:

1.	2nd Lt. Henry H. Arnold	07-05-12
2.	2nd Lt. Thomas DeW. Milling	07-05-12
3.	1st Lt. Benjamin D. Foulois	07-13-12
4.	Capt. Charles deF. Chandler	07-22-12
5.	1st Lt. Paul W. Beck	07-22-12
6.	1st Lt. Harold Geiger	11-20-12
7.	1st Lt. Roy C. Kirtland	01-14-13
8.	1st Lt. Lewis E. Goodier, Jr.	02-14-13
9.	1st Lt. Samuel H. McLeary	03-19-13
10.	2nd Lt. Lewis H. Brereton	04-07-13
11.	1st Lt. Forrest D. Park	05-07-13
12.	1st Lt. Frank P. Lahm	07-14-14
13.	2nd Lt. Carleton G. Chapman	07-19-13
14.	2nd Lt. Herbert A. Dargue	07-19-13
15.	2nd Lt. Eric L. Ellington	09-02-13
16.	2nd Lt. Joseph E. Carberry	09-25-13
17.	2nd Lt. Walter R. Taliaferro	10-15-13
18.	1st Lt. Hugh M. Kelly	11-24-13
19.	2nd Lt. Henry B. Post	11-24-13
20.	2nd Lt. Robert H. Willis, Jr.	12-26-13
21.	2nd Lt. Joseph C. Morrow, Jr.	12-27-13
22.	1st Lt. Townsend F. Dodd	12-30-13
23.	2nd Lt. Fred Seydel	12-31-13
24.	1st Lt. Hollis LeR. Muller	01-15-14
25.	2nd Lt. Douglas B. Netherwood	06-20-14
26.	2nd Lt. Byron Q. Jones	...1914
27.	2nd Lt. Thomas S. Bowman	...1914

THE FIRST NAVAL AVIATORS (USN, USMC, USCG et al) BY NUMBER

This is a listing of 271 aviators who were assigned sequential Naval Aviator numbers. The time period is not known, but appears to be from the pre-1920's perhaps into the 1930's. It encompasses various services as listed. Taken from Office of Naval Operations document of 1960. Asterisk indicated person deceased.

Naval Aviator Number	Name	Service
1	Ellyson, Theodore G.*	USN
2	Rodgers, John*	USN
3	Towers, John H.*	USN
4	Herbster, Victor D.*	USN
5	Cunningham, Alfred A.*	USMC
6	Smith, Bernard L.*	USMC
7	Chevalier, Godfrey deC.*	USN
8	Bellinger, Patrick N. L.	USN
9	Billingsley, William D.*	USN
10	Murray, James M.*	USN
11	Mustin, Henry C.*	USN
12	McIlvain, William M.	USMC
13	Richardson, Holden C.*	USN
14	Saufley, Richard C.*	USN
15	Bronson, Clarence K.*	USN
16	Whiting, Kenneth*	USN
17	Maxfield, Louis H.*	USN
18	McDonnell, Edward O.*	USN
19	Capehart, Wadleigh*	USN
20	Spencer, Earl W., Jr.*	USN
21	Bartlett, Harold T.*	USN
22	Murray, George D.*	USN
23	Corry, William M.*	USN
24	Read, Albert C.	USN
25	Johnson, Earle F.	USN
26	Evans, Francis T.+	USMC
27	Paunack, Robert R.+	USN
28	Schofield, Harold W.	USN
29	Child, Warren G.*	USN
30	Dichman, Grattan C.*	USN
31	Young, Robert T.*	USN
32	Gillespie, George S.	USN
33	Mitscher, Marc A.*	USN
34	Strickland, Glenn B.	USN
35	Monfort, James C.	USN
36	Cabaniss, Robert W.*	USN
37	Chase, Nathan B.*	USN
38	Stone, Elmer F.*	USCG
39	McKitterick, Edward H.	USN
40	Leighton, Bruce G.	USN
41	Griffin, Virgil C.*	USN
42	Cecil, Henry B.*	USN
43	Sugden, Charles E.	USCG
44	Bressman, Augustus A.*	USN
45	Ramsey, DeWitt C.	USN
46	Hull, Carl T.*	USN
47	Peyton, Paul J.*	USN
48	Kirkpatrick, Robert D.	USN
49	Geiger, Roy S.*	USMC
50	Bonner, Walter D.	USN
51	Murphy, Thomas H.	USN
52	Mason, Charles P., Jr.	USN
52fi	Salsman, James	USN
53	Simpson, Frank, Jr.*	NNV
54	Donahue, Robert	USCG
55	Brewster, David L. S.	USMC
55fi	Sundermann, John T.*	USN
56	Barin, Louis T.*	NNV
57	Parker, Stanley V.	USCG
58	Masek, William	USN
59	Coffin, Eugene A.	USCG
60	Eaton, Philip B.	USCG
61	Enos, George*	USN
62	Varini, Giochino	USN
63	Hawkins, Clarence A.	USN
64	Ruttan, Charles E.*	USN

Naval Aviator Number	Name	Service	Naval Aviator Number	Name	Service
65	Gates, Artemus	USNRF	98	Talbot, Andrew B.	USNRF
65fi	Laud-Brown, Wellesley	USNRF	99	Whitehouse, William P.	USNRF
66	Lovett, Robert A.	USNRF	100	Crompton, George	USNRF
67	Ames, Allen W.	USNRF	100fi	Pennoyer, Ralph G.	USN
68	Gould, Earl C. B.	USNRF	100fl	Presley, Russell A.	USMC
69	Walker, Guy A.*	USN	101	Hamlen, Warner L.	USNRF
70	Kilmer, Oliver P.*	USN	102	Little, Charles G.*	USNRF
71	Talbot, Peter	USN	103	Brewer, Arthur D.	USNRF
72	Davison, Henry P.	USNRF	104	Delano, Merrill P.	USNRF
73	Vorys, John M.	USNRF	104fi	Kelly, R.	USN
74	MacLeish, Kenneth A.*	USNRF	105	Landsdowne, Zachary*	USN
75	Beach, Charles F.	USNRF	105fi	Douglas, Gilbert W.	USNRF
76	Farwell, John V.	USNRF	106	Bell, Colley W.	USNRF
77	Sturtevant, Albert D.*	USNRF	107	Chadwick, Noel	USNRF
78	Read, Russell B.	USNRF	108	Ditman, Albert J.	USNRF
79	Brush, Graham M.	USNRF	109	Donnelly, Thorne	NNV
80	James, Oliver B.*	USNRF	110	Carter, R. C.	USNRF
81	Rockefeller, William A.	USNRF	110fi	Allen, Charles L.	USN
82	McIlwaine, Archibald G.*	USNRF	111	Stone, George W.	USN
83	Read, Curtis S.*	USNRF	111fi	Bradford, Doyle	USNRF
83fi	Gartz, Richard C.	USNRF	112	Atwater, William B.	USNRF
84	Ireland, Robert L.	USNRF	112fi	Webster, Clifford L.	USNRF
85	Ingalls, David S.	USNRF	113	Fallon, Nugent*	USNRF
86	Walker, Samuel S.	USNRF	114	Williams, Arthur S.	USNRF
87	Smith, Kenneth R.	USNRF	115	Dietrich, Arthur F.	USN
88	Lynch, Francis R. V.	USNRF	116	Palmer, Carlton D.	USN
89	Lawrence, George F., Jr.	USNRF	117	Murray, Cecil D.	USNRF
89fi	Merrill, Norman E.	NNV	118	Taylor, Moseley	USNRF
90	McLaughlin, Guy*	USN	119	Townsend, Richard S.*	USNRF
91	McCrary, Frank R.*	USN	120	Walton, Mark W.	USNRF
92	Coombe, Reginald G.	USNRF	121	Depew, Ganson G.	USNRF
93	Landon, Henry H., Jr.	USNRF	122	Goodyear, Frank H.	USNRF
94	Culbert, Frederic P.*	USN	123	McCormick, Alexander A.*	USNRF
95	Feher, Anthony	USN	124	Schieffelin, John J.	USNRF
95a	Fitzsimon, R.	Argentina Navy	125	Rodman, Thomas C.	USNRF
			126	Smith, Edward T.	USNRF
95b	Pichon, C. F.	Argentina Navy	127	Otis, James S.	USNRF
			128	Hawkins, Ashton W.	USNRF
95c	Zar, M. A.	Argentina Navy	129	Lufkin, Chauncey F.	USNRF
			130	Potter, Stephen*	USNRF
96	Coil, Emory W.	USN	131	Fuller, Percival S.	USNRF
96fi	Chamberlain, Edmund G.	USMC	132	DeCernea, Edward*	USNRF
97	Strader, Ralph M.*	USNRF	133	Ott, George A.	USN

Naval Aviator Number	Name	Service	Naval Aviator Number	Name	Service
134	Geary, John W.*	USNRF	175	Boyd, Theodore P.	NNV
134fi	Wetherald, Royal W.	USNRF	175fi	Alexander, William H.*	USN
135	Hinton, Walter	USN	176	White, Lawrence G.*	NNV
136	Wilcox, Westmore, Jr.	USNRF	177	Coddington, Dave H.*	NNV
137	Lee, Benjamin, II*	USNRF	178	Kerr, Robert H.*	USN
138	Stone, Emory A.	USNRF	179	Whitted, James A.*	USN
139	Fuller, Charles F.	USNRF	180	Haskell, Amory L.	USNRF
140	Hutchins, Hurd	USNRF	181	Hyde, Russell N.	USNRF
141	Stocker, Robert M.*	USNRF	182	Keyes, Kenneth B.	USNRF
142	Foster, John C.	USNRF	183	Warren, Aldred K., Jr.	USNRF
143	Allen, Frederick S.	USNRF	184	Eaton, Joseph A.	USNRF
144	Amory, Francis I.	USNRF	185	Peterson, William L.*	USNRF
145	Read, Duncan H.	USNRF	186	Stanley, Henry T.	USNRF
146	Goldthwaite, Duval R.*	USNRF	187	Remey, John T.*	USNRF
147	McCann, Richard H.	USNRF	188	Palmedo, Roland	USNRF
148	Wright, Arthur H.*	USNRF	189	Forbes, Duncan P.*	USNRF
149	Swift, Henry	USNRF	190	Allen, Francis G.*	USNRF
150	Butler, Stuart M.*	USNRF	191	Baker, Charles S.	USNRF
151	Gordon, Harry B., Jr.	USNRF	192	Greennough, Charles W.	USNRF
152	Zunino, Frank A., Jr.	USNRF	193	Ames, Charles B.	USNRF
153	Shea, Edward L.	USNRF	194	Hoffer, Richard H.	USNRF
154	Forrestal, James V.*	USNRF	195	Ives, Paul F.*	USNRF
155	Brackenridge, Gavin	USNRF	196	Clark, Robert F.*	USNRF
156	Gibson, Harold F.	USNRF	197	Brewer, Edward S.	USNRF
157	Mudge, William F.	USNRF	198	Dumas, Gardner D.	USNRF
158	Clarkson, William*	USNRF	199	McNamara, John F.*	USNRF
159	McCord, Paul H.	USNRF	200	Rowen, Harold J.	USNRF
160	Halstead, Jacob S.	USNRF	201	Compo, George L.	USNRF
161	Randolph, Robert D.	USNRF	202	Perrin, John	USNRF
162	Matter, Robert	USNRF	203	Hutchinson, Lester B.	USNRF
163	Warburton, William J.	USNRF	204	MacCaulay, Donald M.	USNRF
163fi	Peterson, Harry A.	NNV	205	Lochman, Dean E.*	USNRF
164	Rutherford, John M.	NNV	206	Moore, Lloyd R.	USN
165	Laughlin, George M., III	NNV	207	Thomas, Reginald D.*	USNRF
166	Evans, George B., Jr.*	NNV	208	Clements, James R.	USNRF
167	Johnson, Albert R.*	NNV	209	Schermerhorn, Horace	USNRF
168	McCulloch, David H.	USNRF	210	Murphy, Dudley B.	USNRF
169	Pierce, Thomas J. H.	NNV	210fi	Grosvenor, Theodore P.	USNRF
170	Page, Phillip W.*	USNRF	211	Roe, George T.*	USNRF
171	Shaw, George W.*	USNRF	212	Teulon, Arthur P.	USNRF
172	Peck, Lyman S.*	USNRF	213	Marriner, Walter F.	USN
173	Humphreys, William Y., Jr.*	NNV	214	Pumpelly, Harold A.*	USNRF
174	Berger, Frederick G. B.*	NNV	215	Biggers, Robert L.	USNRF

Naval Aviator Number	Name	Service	Naval Aviator Number	Name	Service
216	Farmer, Charles R.	USNRF	233	Gadsden, Phillip	USNRF
217	Rumill, George E.	USNRF	234	Graves, Justin D.	USNRF
218	Greenfield, Edwin R.	USNRF	235	Connolly, Leo W.	USNRF
219	Weld, Lathrop M.*	USNRF	236	McAdoo, William G., Jr.	USNRF
220	Phelan, James	USNRF	237	Wheeler, Oscar G.	USNRF
220fi	West, Winifred M.	USNRF	238	Benjamin, Henry R.	USNRF
221	Lancto, Joseph W.	USNRF	239	Souther, Arthur F.*	USNRF
222	Wilcox, Howard N.	USNRF	240	Roberts, Charles H., Jr.	USNRF
223	Hawkins, Ress	USNRF	241	Harris, Fred M.	USNRF
224	Wenz, Edward A.	USNRF	242	Naylor, Henry R.	USNRF
225	Alvord, Donald B.	USNRF	243	Voorhees, Dudley A.	USNRF
226	Baum, James E., Jr.	USNRF	244	Maxwell, Howard W., Jr.	USNRF
227	Smith, Frank S.	USNRF	245	King, Frederick E.	USNRF
228	Hawkins, Sam	USNRF	246	Lamar, Lamartine V.	USNRF
229	Clapp, Kenneth H.	USNRF	247	Bancroft, Frederick W.	USNRF
230	Dowell, Benjamin B.*	USNRF	248	Griswold, Rettig A.	USNRF
231	Ostridge, Charles L.*	USNRF	249	Chapman, Thomas H.	USNRF
232	Bergin, Thomas M.	USNRF	250	Frothingham, Phillip B.*	USNRF

Notes: + Awards of the Distinguished Flying Cross.

Service abbreviations:
    USN - Navy
    USMC - Marine Corps
    USCG - Coast Guard
    NNV - National Naval Volunteers (Naval Militia)
    USNRF - Naval Reserve Force

Appendix II

Medal Procurement, Numbering, and Manufacture.

There were a few prototype medals struck in response to direction from the Secretary of the Treasury to the Director of the Mint some time before January 22, 1927, per a letter referring to designs and models. There was no statement as to the quantity. Other information indicates that "models" were sent for review to both the War Department and the Navy Department. The first 10 men awarded the DFC in May 1927 did not receive it until 7 or more months after their certificates had been presented, and one newspaper account indicates that their medals were not ready earlier.

Numbering.
However, in the meantime, 5 medals were presented - the first one (Lindbergh) had an engraved number "1" at the base of the low arm, the next two, to Byrd and Noville, had no number (according to informal data) and the next two had numbers 2 and 3 which could very well have been engraved. The award card for John Benton gives medal number 13. Benton was, in fact, th 13th person presented from the War Department. Subsequent known medals in this time frame had impressed numbers at the base, e.g number 19 for Russell Maughan and number 20 for Hawthorne Gray. At some point, probably between No. 3 and number 19, the War Department would order impressed sequential numbers. Ultimately WD procurements run to an estimated 600 numbered medals. The marking appeared on the base of the lower arm; (possibly some early ones were rim numbered according to unconfirmed data). After 200 it was placed on the rim. The author has personally viewed the reverse of, or a photo print or copy, or has received an official number for 47 medals below number 208. Number 207 is the last known pre December 7, 1941 award. Refer to Appendix IV for known numbers.

Quantities.
There were a total of 16 to 18 crosses presented in 1927 to all services of which 5 or more could have been models. Twelve to fourteen more were issued in 1928. It is reasonable to assume that the initial procurement by the War Department, would have been at least 25 medals, ordered from Bailey Banks and Biddle (BB&B). It is also clear that BB&B made fewer than 43 of the first medals (plus additional unnumbered medals). Sometime in 1927, the WD requested procurement of 150, then canceled and later ordered no more than 50 on February 28, 1929. Indications are that this order, and maybe more, was struck by August C. Frank and covered numbers 43 or lower through 107 or more. An order in c. 1932 was let to Mayer Co., covering at least medals 115 through 136, and were struck without a manufacturer's mark to cover some 30 awards, there must have been more on hand to cover the first few months of 1929 - so perhaps the initial order was for 50. The Navy first requested 2 medals from the WD July 1927, (for Byrd and Noville) then issued a Navy requisition to the WD for 20 DFCs.

Navy requisitions from the WD were: The first two, then the 20 medals on March 9, 1928, 20 on August 18, 1930, 4 medals (numbered 79, 86, 89, and 90) on November 3, 1930 and 25 medals (No. 105 to 129) on February 10, 1932. The Navy thus acquired some 71 of the WD's 200+ stock, leaving some 130 for their 104 awards. Actually, the Navy provided two medals for WD awards - Balbo and Pellegrini. Finally the Navy directly ordered 99 medals plus 2 samples directly from the mint August 4, 1939 - no number information was indicated, but the medals were possibly numbered, and carried on into WWII. However, the author currently believes that only War Department ordered medals were numbered.

Manufacturer.
Manufacturer is also a difficult issue. WD medals No. 1, 19, and 20 are Bailey, Banks and Biddle (BB&B), and should clearly extend to all between. If 50 medals was the initial procurement quantity, then medal No. 43 should not be August Frank (Aug. C. Frank) which it is. No.43 is unnamed and most likely unissued unless it occurred after its photo was taken (National Archives). So possibly the WD procured 40

medals (plus or minus some which may include the models) from BB&B, then some quantity from Frank. No. 62 and 80 are reported as August Frank, and 105 is. No. 99 has no maker's mark and numbers in the 100's are reported with no maker's hallmark, e.g. 116,136 and 198. It is also possible that there were two sets of numbers. The author only has one reported case of a duplicate occurring, and has not confirmed the accuracy of this report.

Naming of DFCs.
To date, the research for this era indicates that the War Department issued medals that carried the first name, initial, and last name of the awardee as general policy. The Navy policy was to carry as many as seven or eight lines including; From the President, rank, names, dates, action, etc. I have yet to find any exceptions, although admittedly the examples are still few and far between. These tended to carry on into World War II, but there may be deviations in both services.

There must be many collectors who have more information on this than the author, who would be interested in learning any of it.

Appendix III
Other Awards of Some DFC Winners

Military Decorations of Brigadier General Herbert A. Dargue (born 17 November, 1886, in Brooklyn, New York; died 12 December, 1941 because of an airplane crash near Bishop, California; buried at Arlington National Cemetery, Section 7).
1. U.S. Distinguished Flying Cross
2. Army Mexican Service Medal. He served as a member of the 1st Aero Squadron under Captain Benjamin D. Foulois during the Mexican Punitive Expedition of 1916 to 1917.
3. World War I Victory Medal
4. American Defense Service Medal
5. Venezuelan Order of the Liberator
6. Order of the Sun of Peru
7. Bolivian Order of the Condor of the Andes
8. Chilean Order of Merit

Military Decorations of General Arthur B. McDaniel.
1. U.S. Distinguished Flying Cross
2. World War I Victory Medal
3. Army of Occupation of Germany
4. American Defense Medal, with one Bronze Service Star
5. American Campaign Medal
6. Service Medal
7. World War II Victory Medal
8. Venezuelan Order of the Liberator (also known as the Order of the Bust of Bolivar)
9. Order of the Sun of Peru
10. Bolivian Order of the Condor of the Andes
11. Chilean Order of Merit
12. Order of the Crown of Italy. Awarded by the Italian King in recognition of services to General Italo Balbo's Aerial Cruise to America
13. Peruvian Aviation Cross 1st Class
    Papers indicate that neither he, or his next of kin, ever received the actual decoration from Peru

Military Decorations of General Ira C. Eaker.
1. Army Distinguished Service Medal, with two OLC's
2. Navy Distinguished Service Medal
3. Silver Star
4. Legion of Merit
5. U.S. Distinguished Flying Cross with one Bronze Oak Leaf Cluster
6. Air Medal
7. World War I Victory Medal
8. American Defense Service Medal with one Bronze Servie Star
9. European-African-Middle Eastern Campaign Medal with "Arrowhead" device and two Silver Service Stars
10. World War II Victory Medal
11. Order of the Bath
12. British Empire Medal
13. Bolivian Order of the Condor of the Andes
14. Brazilian Order of the Southern Cross
15. Brazilian Order of Aeronautical Merit
16. Chilean Order of Merit
17. French Legion of Honor
18. French Croix de Guerre (WWII)
19. Italian Order of Saint Maurice and Saint Lazurus
20. Order of the Sun of Peru
21. Polish Cross of Merit
22. Soviet Order of Kutuzov
23. Venezuelan Order of the Liberator
24. Yugoslavian Order of the Partisan Star

Awards of General Muir S. Fairchild.
1. Army Distinguished Service Medal
2. Legion of Merit
3. U.S. Distinguished Fllying Cross
4. Purple Heart (World War I wound)
5. Mexican Border Service Medal
6. World War I Victory Medal with four Bronze Service Stars
7. American Defense Service Medal
8. American Campaign Medal
9. World War II Victory Medal

10. French *Croix de Guere* (World War I award) with Bronze Star (denoting mention in dispatches).
11. Italian War Medal (World War I award)
12. Venezuelan Order of the Liberator
13. Order of the Sun of Peru
14. Bolivian Order of the Condor of the Andes
15. Chilean Order of Merit

Awards to Captain Hauptman Herman Koehl.
1. Prussian Pour le Merite ("Blue Max") as WWI Bomber pilot
2. Prussian Knight's Cross with swords of the Royal Hohenzollem House Order
3. Prussian Iron Cross, first and second class
4. Knight's Cross with Swords of the Order of the Wurttemberg Military Merit Order (only aviation award of this highest award of this state)
5. Knight's Cross of the Wuerttemburg Military Order
6. Knights Cross 1st Class with Swords of the Wuerttemburg Friedrich
7. Austrian Millitary Merit Cross 3rd Class with War Decoration
8. (U.S.) Distinguished Flying Cross
9. Wound Badge (black)

Lieutenant General Ralph J. Mitchell, USMC .
1. DSM Navy and Army
2. Legion of Merit with Gold Star
3. Distinguished Flying Cross
4. WWI Victory
5. 2nd Nicaraguan
6. American Defense Service
7. American Campaign
8. Asiatic-Pacific
9. WWII Victory
10. Philippine Liberation
11. British Companion of the Bath
12. Nicaragua Medal of Merit

Dates of rank of the 10 Pan-Am fliers as of December 1928 (the date the flight began) and 1943 *Official Army* for the 10 men.

    Major Herbert A. Dargue (SVC #03084) 1 July 1920
    Captain Arthur B. McDaniel (SVC #07269) 1 July i920
    Captain Ira C. Eaker (SVC #07478) 1 July 1920
    Captain Clinton F. Woolsey (SVC #08352) 17 September 1925
    First Lieutenant Leonard D. Weddington (SVC #011313) 1July 1920
    First Lieutenant Bernard S. Thompson (SVC #010704) 1 July 1920
    Second Lieutenant Charles McK. Robinson (SVC #010735) April 1920
    Second Lieutenant Muir S. Fairchild (SVC #010555)
    Second Lieutenant Ennis C. Whitehead (SVC #010572)
    Second Lieutenant John W. Benton (SVC #010983)

APPENDIX IV
KNOWN NUMBERED DFCs, PRE- AND EARLY WORLD WAR II

Name	Award Number*	Medal Number**	Maker	Date Presented
Charles Lindbergh	11	1 (engraved)	BB&B	06-11-27
Richard E. Byrd	1st USN	NONE	BB&B	07-19-27
Lester Maitland	(12)	(2)		09-29-27
Albert Hegenberger	13	3		09-29-27
Ira C. Eaker	3	NONE	BB&B	12-21-27
John Benton	10	13		03-10-28
Russell Maughan	18	19	BB&B	08-06-28
Hawthorne Gray	14	20 pearl catch box	BB&B	08-29-28
no name (per A. Gleim)		21	BB&B	
Benjamin Mendez (Colu.)	36	22	BB&B	03-07-30
Dieudonne Costes (France)		24	BB&B	08-29-29
Uzal G. Ent	32	30		06-25-29
Ross C. Kirkpatrick	26	32		04-19-29
Joseph English	30	33		06-25-29
Eric H. Nelson	29	34		08-06-29
James D. Long	31	35		04-11-29
Clifford C. Nutt	27	36		04-04-29
Clarence E. Crumrine	28	37		04-16-29
Elwood R., Quesada	39	38		03-02-29
Wilbur Wright	34	NONE - Civ.	BB&B	02-27-29
Carl Spaatz	37	40		03-02-29
no name, (National Archives)		43	A.Frank	
Thomas Turner		48 USMC		08-16-29
Louis Bourne		59 USMC	A.Frank	1928/29?
Lawson Sanderson		62 USMC		08-31-29
Ross E. Rowell		63 USMC	A.Frank	09-07-28
Lowell H. Smith	42	64	A.Frank	11-04-29
John F. Richter	43	65	A.Frank	08-28-29
Dean C. Smith	47	72		07-09-30
Ashley C. McKinley	46	73		07-09-30
+Claude Alexander		79 USN		12-20-30
Gordon W. Heritage		80 USMC	A.Frank	mid 1932?

Name	Award Number*	Medal Number**	Maker	Date Presented
+Patrick A. McDonough		86 USN		late 1930?
+Thomas G. Reid		89 USN		late 1930
+William J. Murtha		90 USN		11-29-30
Roger M. Ramey (Wake Island)		99	none	1942
Exhibition Only		102	A.Frank	
no name (Private Collector)		++105	A.Frank	
Eugene B. Ely		++107 Civilian	A.Frank	02-16-33
Tbd, 8th AF		++111		09- -42
Joseph A. Pelter		++115 USN	none	1936?
Neal G. Williams		++116 USMC	none	05-18-33
Amelia Earhart Putnam	56	131 Civilian	none	07-29-32
Harold Gatty	59	132 Civilian		08-18-32
John L. Polando	58	133 Civilian		07-28-32
Russell N. Boardman	57	134 Civilian		07-28-32
Wiley Post	60	135 Civilian		08-18-32
no name		136	none	
Richard T. Aldworth		167	A.Frank	06-05-37
W.N. Davis		194 USN		1944
no name, Blakeney (Dept. of Heraldry)		198	none	
William Hudnell		207 rim	none	03-07-41
no name (per A. Gleim)		209 rim	none	
no name		210		
Gordon H. Sterling Jr.		223***		08-28-42
Cecil L. Faulkner		224		08-28-42
Walter K. Heitzman		225		08-28-42
William B. Compton		226		08-28-42
Thomas C. Mustain		227		08-28-42
Simpson L. Jennings		228		08-28-42
Benjamin Clifton		229		08-28-42
Jerome G. Parsons		230		08-28-42
Joseph A. Caputo		231		08-28-42
Robert Johns		232		08-28-42
no name		298 rim	BB&B	
no name		308	BB&B	
Erwin J Dobberpfuhl(Pearl Catch Box)		561 rim		Sept.'41 flight

*Award Numbers are as recorded for War Department Awards on award cards. There were a total of 104 War Department awards found by the author not counting second or third awards. Award cards for a total of 80 persons were received, of these 71 carried an Award Number. These ranged from Herbert Dargue, number 1, to Thomas O'Malley number 100.

Only 19 cards had a DFC number noted on them, starting with No. 3 for Albert Hegenberger to 135 for Wiley Post. Of 19 USN cards/certificates received, none had any numbering data nor any significant dates.

**War Department awards to Army Air Force unless noted - date, in most cases, is date of presentation.

+The USN requisitioned four medals from the War Department for enlisted personnel, which probably are these four, possibly in some other order.

++ Numbers 105 through 129 were requisitioned by the USN from stock purchased from War Department.

Note: Photographs or photocopies of the several early medals show the following: Admiral Byrd's DFC, presented just after Lindbergh's, shows BB&B Bronze but no number. Ira Eaker's DFC, which should be No. 6, was not stamped on the reverse. It has not been examined for rim marking. It is marked BB&B Bronze. Orville and Wilbur Wright's medals presented just before Carl Spaatz, 1929, have no number and are marked BB&B Bronze.

***The sequence of numbers from 223 to 232 for Aug. 28, 1942 were awarded in Hawaii for Pearl Harbor citations.

OAK LEAF CLUSTER AWARDS, 1927 to WWII:

NAME	GENERAL ORDERS	PRESENTED
1. Ira C. Eaker	7, 1929	06-06-29
2. James Doolittle	16, 1929	10-25-29
3. Albert Hegenberger	1, 1934	tbd
4. Albert Stevens	4, 1936	05-12-36
5. Orville Anderson	4, 1936	03-07-36
6. Caleb V. Haynes	5, 1942	03-28-42
7. tbd		
8. Caleb V. Haynes (2nd)	19, 1942	04-05-43

RIBBON STYLES (Observed from medals or Photos of above).
Medal Numbers 1, 19, 20, 59, 63, 80, 99, 105, split (half-wrap) brooch
Medal Numbers 116 and 131 full-wrap brooch
Medal Numbers 207 and 210, split (half-wrap) brooch

DATA SOURCES:
Award cards, photographs and communications from museums, and from personal collections, and communications from members of OMSA.

APPENDIX V - INDEX OF DFC AWARDS - WAR DEPARTMENT
DISTINGUISHED FLYING CROSS - FIRST GENERAL ORDER RELEASES 1927/1941
WD and ACT of CONGRESS

NAME	RANK	EVENT	DATES S. of WAR APPR.	CERTIF. ISSUE	MEDAL AWARD	NUMBERS ON AWARD CARD	MEDAL	OTHER AWARDS/NOTES
GENERAL ORDERS No. 6, MAY 18, 1927 PAN-AMERICAN GOODWILL FLIGHT OF FIVE AIRCRAFT								
Benton, John W.[1]	1st Lt.	02-26-27	05-02-27	05-02-27	03-10-28[2]	10	13	
Dargue, Herbert A.	Maj.	05-02-27	05-02-27	05-02-27	12-21-27	1		Officer, Order of Merit
Eaker, Ira C.[3]	Capt.	05-02-27	05-02-27	05-02-27	12-21-27	3		C.G. VIIIAF, Off. Ord. of Merit
Fairchild, Muir S.	1st Lt.	05-02-27	05-02-27	05-02-27	12-21-27	7		COM,Purple Heart,Cr.deGuerre
McDaniel, Arthur B.	Capt.	05-02-27	05-02-27	05-02-27	12-21-27	2		
Robinson, Charles McK.	1st Lt.	05-02-27	05-02-27	05-02-27	12-21-27	6		COM,, (Certificate of Merit)
Thompson, Bernard S.	1st Lt.	05-02-27	05-02-27	05-02-27	12-21-27	5		
Weddington, Leonard D.	1st Lt.	05-02-27	05-02-27	05-02-27	12-21-27	4		
Whitehead, Ennis C.	1st Lt.	05-02-27	05-02-27	05-02-27	12-21-27	8		COM
Woolsey, Clinton F.[1]	Capt.	02-26-27	05-02-27	05-02-27	06-28-28[3]	(9)		
GENERAL ORDERS No. 8, JUNE 4, 1927 NEW YORK TO PARIS FLIGHT (RUSH ORDER, 06-02-27)								
Lindbergh, Charles A.	Capt.	05-21-27	06-01-27	06-11-27	06-11-27	(11)	1	Pres. by Coolidge MoH 12-14-27
GENERAL ORDERS No. 16, OCTOBER 22, 1927 OAKLAND TO HONOLULU FLIGHT								
Hegenberger, Albert F.[3]	1st Lt.	06-29-27	07-14-27	07-21-27	09-29-27	13	3	Gr. Off. Ord. Crown, Italy
Maitland, Lester J.	1st Lt.	06-29-27	07-14-27		09-29-27	(12)	2	

NAME	RANK	EVENT	S. of WAR APPR.	CERTIF. ISSUE	MEDAL AWARD	NUMBERS ON AWARD CARD	MEDAL	OTHER AWARDS/NOTES
GENERAL ORDERS No. 4, MARCH 31, 1928								
Goebel, Arthur C.	2nd Lt.	08-17-27	02-18-28	04-11-28	08-17-28	15		Dole Flight to Hawaii
Kelly, Oakley G.	1st Lt.	05-03-23	02-18-28			17		New York to Coronado
MacReady, John A.	1st Lt.	05-03-23	02-18-28		07-28-28	18		New York to Coronado
Maughan, Russell L.	1st Lt.	06-23-24	02-18-28		08-06-28		19	DSC, N.Y. to San Francisco
GENERAL ORDERS No. 5, APRIL 14, 1928 HIGH ALTITUDE BALLOON FLIGHT								
Gray, Hawthorne C.[1,4]	Capt.	3,5,11,27	02-18-28	04-13-28	08-29-28[2]	14	20	High altitude ballon flights
GENERAL ORDERS No. 14, OCTOBER 8, 1928 - 05-02-28 AWARDS by ACT of CONGRESS P. 341								
Costes, Dieudonne (Fr.)	Lt.	02- -28	05-02-28		08-29-29	(23)	24	Paris to U.S. 35,000 miles
Crumrine, Clarence E.	2nd Lt.	10-20-20	08-18-28	01-11-29	04-16-29	28	37	Alaska Expedition, 1920
de Pinedo, Francesco (It.)	Col.	03- -27	05-02-28	10-12-28	10-12-28	22		Rome to US, 25,000 mi.
English, Joseph E.	MSgt.	10-20-20	08-18-28	01-11-20	06-25-29	30	33	Alaska Expedition, 1920
Ent, Uzal G.[4]	2nd Lt.	05-30-28	09-11-28	01-11-29	06-25-29	32	30	Balloonist, CG 9th AF, (WWII)
Fitzmaurice, James C. (Eire) Maj.		04-13-28	05-02-28	05-02-28	05-02-28	20		1st West. trans-Atlantic to U.S.
Kirkpatrick, Ross C.[1]	1st Lt.	10-20-20	08-18-28	01-11-29	04-19-29[2]	26		Alaska Expedition, 1920
Koehl, Hermann (Ger.)	Capt.	04-13-28	05-02-28	05-02-28	05-02-28	21		1st West. trans-Atlantic to U.S.
LeBrix, Joseph (Fr.)	Lt. Cmdr.	02- -28	05-02-28		09-28-28	24		So. Atlantic 35,000 mi. to U.S.
Long, James D.	Sgt.	10-20-20	08-18-28		04-11-29	31	35	Alaska Expedition, 1920
Nelson, Eric H.	1st Lt.	10-20-20	08-18-28	01-11-29	08-06-29	29	34	DSM (WWI), Alaska Expd. '20
Nutt, Clifford C.	1st Lt.	10-20-20	08-18-28	01-11-29	04-04-29	27	36	Alaska Expd. 1920
Street, St. Clair	1st Lt.	10-20-20	08-18-28	01-11-29	10-08-28	25		PHrt. Alaska Expd. '20
Von Huenefeld, Gunther (Ger.) Baron		04-13-28	05-02-28	05-02-28	05-02-28	19		1st West. trans-Atlantic to U.S.

NAME	RANK	EVENT	DATES S. of WAR APPR.	CERTIF. ISSUE	MEDAL AWARD	NUMBERS ON AWARD CARD	MEDAL	OTHER AWARDS/NOTES
GENERAL ORDERS No. 3, 1929 ALASKA TO SPITZBERGEN, 2,200 MILES								
Eielson, Carl B.	1st Lt.	04-16-28	12-09-28		02-01-29	(33)		Also Harmon Trophy Winner
GENERAL ORDERS No. 7, 1929 INCLUDES OLC								
Eaker, Ira C.	Capt.	01-07-29	03-02-29	03-29-29	04-06-29	OLC #1		150-hour refueling flight
Halverson, Harry A.	1st Lt.	01-07-29	03-02-29	03-30-29	07-13-29	38		150-hour refueling flight
Hook, Ray W.	SSgt.	01-07-29	03-02-29		03-02-29	(40)		150-hour refueling flight
Quesada, Elwood R.	1st Lt.	01-07-29	03-02-29	03-30-29	03-02-29	39	38	150-hour refueling flight
Spaatz, Carl	Maj.	01-07-29	03-02-29	03-30-29	03-02-29	37	40	DSC,CG VIII AF, pre-Doolittle
Wright, Oliver	Civ.	12-17-03	12-18-28	02-27-29	02-27-29	(35)	none	Kitty Hawk flight
Wright, Wilbur[1]	Civ.	12-17-03	12-18-28	02-27-29	02-27-29	34	none	Kitty Hawk flight
GENERAL ORDERS No. 12, 1929								
Mendez, Benjamin (Col.)	Capt.	12-30-28	03-01-29	05-08-29	03-07-30	36	22	N.Y.C. to Columbia, 4600 mi.
Smith, Ernest L.	2nd Lt./Capt.	07-15-27	03-06-29	03-24-29	08-16-29	41		Oakland, CA to Molokai, I II
GENERAL ORDERS No. 16, 1929 INCLUDES OLC to DOOLITTLE for 3- 24 FLIGHT TEST; (MoH 5-19-42 for TOKYO)								
Doolittle, James H.[3]	1st Lt.	09-05-22	07-02-29	10-21-29	10-25-29	44		FL. to CA, C.G VIII AF, MoH
Doolittle, James H.	1st Lt.	03- ? -24	07-02-29	10-21-29	10-25-29	OLC #2		Flight testing
Richter, John P.	1st Lt.	06-29-23	07-02-29	10-21-29	08-28-29	43	65	37-hour flight with refueling
Smith, Lowell H.	1st Lt.	06-29-23	07-02-29	10-21-29	11-04-29	42	64	as above, DSM –
Sutton, Harry A.	1st Lt.	12-22-26	07-02-29	10-21-29	08-28-29	45		Flight tests at Santa Monica,CA

NAME	RANK	EVENT	S. of WAR APPR.	CERTIF. ISSUE	MEDAL AWARD	AWARD CARD	MEDAL	OTHER AWARDS/NOTES
GENERAL ORDERS No. 2, 1931								
Jones, Ulysses G.[4]	1st Lt.	05-14-30	09-05-30	09-12-30	10-30-30	48		Sea rescue assistance, Hawaii
McKinley, Ashley C.	Capt.	1928/30	07-03-30	07-18-30	07-09-30	46	73	Byrd Antarctic/So. Pole Exped.
Meyer, Walter T.[4]	1st Lt.	05-14-30	09-05-30	09-12-30	10-30-30	49		Sea rescue assistance Hawaii
Rawlings, Edwin W.[4]	2nd Lt.	05-14-30	09-05-30	09-12-30	10-30-30	50		Sea rescue assistance Hawaii
Smith, Dean Cull	2nd Lt.	1928/30	07-03-30	07-18-30	07-09-30	47	72	Byrd Antarctic/So. Pole Exped.
Summers, Robert F.[4]	SSgt.	05-14-30	09-05-30	09-12-30	12-19-30	51		Sea rescue assistance Hawaii
GENERAL ORDERS No. 6, 1931 TO CARRY OUT SECRET ORDERS ON FLIGHT TO VANCOUVER THEN NEWARK, NJ								
Caldwell, William W.[1,4]	2nd Lt.	10-15-30	03-12-31	02-02-32	05-01-31	52		Bad weather emergency flight
Woodring, Irvin A.[4]	2nd Lt.	10-16-30	03-12-31	01-13-32	04-16-31	53		Bad weather emergency flight
GENERAL ORDERS No. 2 & No. 6, 1932								
Moor, Robert D.[1,4]	1st Lt.	08-23-31	12-22-31	09-29-32	02-06-32	54		Saved life after collision
Neff, Frank D.[4]	Sgt.	12-04-31	03-31-32	09-29-32	05-26-32	55		Saved dirigible and crew
GENERAL ORDERS No. 4, 1933 ACT OF CONGRESS PUB. 31 7-11-32, 7-2-32 for PUTMAN								
Boardman, Russell N.	Civ.	07-30-31	07-11-32	07-28-32	07-28-32	57	134	U.S. to Istanbul, 5000 mi.
Gatty, Harold	Civ.	07-01-31	07-11-32	08-18-32	08-18-32	59	132	Around-the-World
Polando, John L.	Civ.	07-30-31	07-11-32	07-28-32	07-28-32	58	133	U.S. to Istanbul, 5000 mi.
Post, Wiley	Civ.	07-01-31	07-11-32	08-18-32	08-18-32	60	135	Around-the-World
Putnam, Amelia Earhart	Civ.	05-20-32	07-02-32	07-29-32	07-29-32	56	131	Newfoundland to Eire

NAME	RANK	EVENT	S. of WAR APPR.	CERTIF. ISSUE	MEDAL AWARD	AWARD MEDAL CARD	OTHER AWARDS/NOTES
GENERAL ORDERS No. 6, 1933, *ACT OF CONGRESS FOR CURTISS*, 3-1-32							
Bottriell, Ralph W.	MSgt.	05-19-19			01- ? -33		1st free parachute jumps
Bruner, Donald L.	Capt.		06-01-33	10-24-33	06-28-33	63	Night flying development
Curtiss, Glenn H.[1]	Civ.	years	03-01-33		06-12-33		Advancing aero science
GENERAL ORDERS No. 1, 1934							
Hegenberger, Albert F.	Capt.	05-09-32	02-13-34	05-18-34		OLC #3	Instrument flt/landing tests
SPECIAL ACTS							
Bronte, Emory B.	Civ.	07-15-27	06-18-34		11-04-34		2nd Calif. to Hawaii flight
Balbo, Italo	Gen. Italy	08-12-33	03-10-35		06-15-35?		Led 25 planes to Chicago
Pellegrini, Aldo	Gen. Italy	08-12-33	03-10-35	07-15-35	4 to 7-35		Led 25 planes to Chicago
GENERAL ORDERS No. 8, 1934 (1); No. 3, 1935 (4); No. 8, 1935 (1); No. 4, 1936 (1) and OLCs (2)							
Meredith, Russell L.[4]	1st Lt.	02-07-23	03-17-34		04-24-34		Rescue of injured man
Anderson, Frederick L., Jr[4]	1st Lt.	12-14-34	05-18-35	02-14-36	07-03-35		Near crash in San Francisco
Cousland, Cornelius W.[4]	1Lt./Capt.	05-31-34	09-24-34	11-17-34	01-02-35		Flight failure/safe landing
Anderson, Orville A.[3]	Capt.	07-28-34	10-17-34	11-12-34	12-15-34		Explorer I, 60,000 ft.
Anderson, Orville A.	Capt.	11-11-35	02-06-36	06-24-36	03-07-36	OLC #5	Expl, II, 72,000 ft.
Kepner, William E.	Maj.	07-28-34	10-17-34	11-12-34	12-06-34		Expl., WW1 DSC, VIII Ftr.
Stevens, Albert W.[3]	Capt.	07-28-34	10-17-34	11-12-34	12-06-34		Explorer I, 60,000 ft.
Stevens, Albert W.	Capt.	11-11-35	02-06-36	06-24-36	05-12-36	OLC #4	Explorer II, 70,000 ft.
McDuff, Francis H.[4]	Cadet	06-22-35	08- -35?				Saved lives, aircraft fire

NAME	RANK	EVENT	S. of WAR APPR.	CERTIF. ISSUE	MEDAL AWARD	AWARD CARD	MEDAL	OTHER AWARDS/NOTES
GENERAL ORDERS No. 1, 1937								
Aldworth, Richard T.[4]	1st Lt.	12-12-26	11-27-36	03-06-37	06-05-37		167	Engine failure
Arnold, Henry H.	Lt./Col.	08-20-34	11-25-36	03-06-37	01-05-37	74		10 plane flt., C.G.USAAF
Buckman, Donald W.[1,4]	1Lt./Capt.	11-12-35	10-21-36	03-06-37	02-10-37[2]	79		Landing after heart attack
Connor, Frank B.	Corp.	02-09-36	11-25-36	03-06-37	04-27-37	78		Rescue of CCC crew
Giles, Barney M.	Capt.	02-09-36	11-25-36	03-06-37	04-27-37	75		Rescue of CCC crew
Griffith, John S.[4]	Capt.	07-22-36	10-21-36	03-06-37	02-20-37			Saving crew in flight test
Hamilton, Donald E.	SSgt.	02-09-36	11-25-36	03-06-37	04-27-37	77		Rescue of CCC crew
Irvin, Frank G.[4]	Capt.	07-22-36	10-21-36	03-06-37	12-10-36			Saving crew in flight test
McClellan, Hez[1]	Capt.	-1935-	06-15-36	06-24-36	10-26-36[2]	71		Wash. D.C. to Alaska.
Patrick, James H., Jr.	2nd Lt.	02-09-36	11-25-36	03-06-37	04-27-37	76		Rescue of CCC crew
GENERAL ORDERS No. 5, 1937 PASSENGER EVACUATION AND SAFE LANDING OF DISABLED AIRCRAFT								
Armstrong, Frank A., Jr.[4]	1st Lt.	11-20-35	05-18-37	09-03-37	07-10-37	82		In-flt. Emergency/landing
Wallace, James H.[4]	1st Lt.	11-20-35	05-18-37	09-03-37	07-17-37	81		(same), WWI award
GENERAL ORDERS No. 1, 1938 (INCLUDED IN SUPPLEMENT II, AMERICAN DECORATIONS.)								
Boushey, Homer A., Jr.[4]	2nd Lt.	10-05-36	02-03-38	06-16-38	04-06-38	85		In-flight failure/landing
Ellis, Dross[4]	2nd Lt.	04-24-37	12-21-37	02-11-38	02-12-38	83		Saved pilotless plane
Kelsey, Benjamin S.[4]	1st Lt.	12-24-36	02-03-38	06-16-38	03-09-38	84		Engine failure, fire
SUPPLEMENT II, AMERICAN DECORATIONS JULY 1, 1937 - JUNE 30, 1938								
Olds, Robert	Lt./Col.	02-27-38	04-12-38	06-16-38	04-30-38	86		Mercy flight to Chile

| NAME | RANK | EVENT | DATES | | | NUMBERS ON | | OTHER AWARDS/NOTES |
			S. of WAR APPR.	CERTIF. ISSUE	MEDAL AWARD	AWARD CARD	MEDAL	
SUPPLEMENT III, AMERICAN DECORATIONS JULY 1, 1938 - JUNE 30, 1938								
Haynes, Caleb V.	Capt./Maj.	02-06-39	02-09-39	12-02-39	02-14-39	87		OLC #6 & #8 Mercy flight
Wolfe, Franklin C.	Capt.	02-13-39			07-07-39			Chile Mercy flights
SUPPLEMENT IV, AMERICAN DECORATIONS JULY 1, 1939 - JUNE 30, 1940								
Crane, Carl J.	Capt.	35/37						Development of auto land.
Greene, Carl F.	Maj.	2 yrs.						Cabin pressure tests
Hine, Virgil[1]	1st Lt.	06-29-23	04-30-40					In-flight refueling tests
Holloman, George V.	Capt.	35/37	07-10-39	07-27-39	07-15-39	91		Development of auto land.
Johnson, Alfred H.	Capt.	2 yrs.						Cabin pressure tests
Seifert, Frank W.	1st Lt.	06-29-23	04-30-40					In-flight refueling tests
SUPPLEMENT V, AMERICAN DECORATIONS JULY 1, 1940 - JUNE 30, 1941								
Harris, Samuel R., Jr.	Capt.	4 1/2 yrs.	07-31-40	09-11-40	09-24-40	95		Test pilot career
Hudnell, William T., Jr.[4]	1st Lt.	04-23-40 (NA)			03-07-41		207	Avoid crash in populated area
Lazarus, Willard, W.	2nd Lt.	03-05-40	12-23-40	05-28-41	01-17-41	99		Engine failure, saved crew
Neely, Harold L.[4]	1st Lt.	12-18-39						In-flight aircraft failure
O'Malley, Thomas F.	Sgt.	03-05-40	12-23-40		01-17-41	100		In-flight emerg./WWI Cite.
Price, George E.	Capt.	01-06-40						Aircraft malfunction
Whitney, Raymond U.[4]	Pvt.	2 yrs.	07-31-40	09-11-40	09-24-40	97		Medical corps experiments
Eubeck, Eugene L.	Col.	10-17-41	12-25-41					Refer to Mingo
O'Donnell, Emmett, Jr.	Maj.	09-11-41	12-24-41					Refer to Mingo

OLC AWARD DATA

1. Ira C. Eaker — G.O. No. 7 — W.D 1929 — Question Mark flight
2. James H. Doolittle — G.O. No. 16 — WD 1929 — Aerobatic testing
3. Albert F. Hegenberger — G.O. No. 1 — tbd — Instrument flight and landing
4. Albert W. Stevens — G.O. No. 4 — WD 1936 — Explorer II flight
5. Orville A. Anderson — G.O. No. 4 — WD 1936 — Explorer II flight
6. Caleb V. Haynes — G.O. No. 5 — WD 1942 — (Post Pearl Harbor) Flight to wartime Scotland, July 1941
8. Caleb V. Haynes — G.O. No. 19 — WD 1942 — (Post Pearl Harbor) Flight to Iraq, August/October 1941

1 Posthumous
2 Presented to widow
3 Also OLC Winner
4 Heroism

APPENDIX VI - INDEX OF DFC AWARDS U.S. NAVY, USMC, USCG
SEQUENCE OF AWARDS ESTIMATED BY DATE AND DATA

U.S. NAVY

NAME	RANK	EVENT	APPR.	DATE CERTIF. ISSUE	MEDAL PRES.	NUMBER OF AWARD	MEDAL	EVENT/NOTES
Byrd, Richard Evelyn, Jr.	Cdr.	07-01-27	07-13-27		07-19-27	1		Atlantic crossing
Noville, George O.	Lt.	07-01-27	07-13-27		07-19-27	2		Atlantic crossing
Wyatt, Ben Harrison	Lt.	1926	08-02-27	09-16-27?	09- -27?	3		Alaska Survey C.O.
Cornwell, Delbert Strother [1]	Lt. jg	11-18-26	08-02-27	09-16-27	08-31-29	4		Air accident/rescue
Paunack, Robert Rudolph [1]	Lt. Cdr.	06-03-19	12-13-27		'27/28	5		Extinguish Dirigible fire
Davis, William Virginius, Jr.	Lt.	08-16-27	05-09-28		08-31-29	6		Dole flight co-pilot
Williams, Alford J.	Lt.	05-10-28	05-16-29		05-17-29	7		Inverted flight tests
Cuddihy, George Thomas [2]	Lt.	08-07-29			03-24-30	8		Flight tests/Spinning
Soucek, Apollo	Lt.	05-08-29		10-27-30[4]	12-20-30	9		High altitude flight exper.
Dillon, Wallace M.	Lt.	1926		10-27-30	11-29-30	10		Alaska exped. exec.
Burkett, Eugene F.	Lt.	1926	06-09-30	10-27-30	11-29-30	11		Alaska exped. navigator
Whitehead, Richard F.	Lt. Cdr.	1926	06-09-30	10-27-30	11-29-30	12		Alaska exped. - photo officer
Alexander, Claude George [1]	CRe	1926	06-09-30	10-27-30	12-20-30	13	79[3]	Alaska surv. mechanic
McDonough, Patrick Andrew	CPh	1926	06-09-30		11-29-30	14	86[3]	Alaska survey photography
Reid, Thomas George [2]	CAP	1926	06-09-30		11-29-30	15	89[3]	Alaska Survey - pilot
Murtha, William Joseph	Ph1C	1926	06-09-30		11-29-30	16	90[3]	Alaska survey photography
June, Harold Irving	CAP	11-29-29				17		Byrd Antarctic I pilot
Shoemaker, J. M.	Lt. Cdr.	1927				18		Carrier Franklin, 1944
Ely, Eugene B. [2]	Civ.	1910-11			02-16-33	19	107	Pioneer civilian aviator
Cavin, Doyle J.	AMM2C	12-14-33	02-08-33		07-28-34	20		Saved plane from crash
Bowlin, William Milton	ACMM	11-18-34			03-13-36	21		Byrd Antartcic II pilot
Pelter, Joseph Arnold	Ph1C	11-11-34				22	115	Antarctic II photo maps

NAME	RANK	EVENT	APPR.	DATE CERTIF. ISSUE	MEDAL PRES.	NUMBER OF AWARD MEDAL	EVENT/NOTES
U.S. NAVY							
Akers, Frank L.	Lt.	07-30-35				23	Blind Carrier Landing
McGinnis, Knefler	Lt./Cdr.	10-9-35	04-10-36		04-18-36	24	Norfolk - Canal Zone
Hatfield, Vernon Owen[1]	ACMM	02-02-38				25	Crew rescue in crash
McKay, Donald Bernard[1]	ACMM	02-02-38				26	Crew rescue in crash
Phelps, Otto Russell	RM2C	09-22-38	04-01-39			27	Landed plane w/o pilot
Eoff, James H.[1,2]	Ens.	08-31-39				28	Stayed with plane
Perce, Earle Baker	CRa	1939/41				29	Antarctic discovery flights
Snow, Ashley Clinton	ACMM	1939/41				30	Antarctic discovery flights
Lowrey, William W.[1]	Lt.	05-15-41			06-05-41	31	In-flight rescue
McCants, John Raymond[1]	ACMM	05-15-41			06-05-41	32	In-flight rescue
Rosendahl, Charles L.[1]	RAdm.	09-03-25	06-30-47		1947	33	Shenandoah heroism
U.S. MARINE CORPS							
Rowell, Ross Erastus[1]	Maj.	07-16-27	11-02-27		09-07-28	1	Nicaragua Ocatal flight
Boyden, Hayne D.[1] (099)	1st Lt.	07-16-27	12-21-27			2	Nicaragua, troop rescue
Turner, Thomas C.	Lt. Col.	04-22-21	12-13-27		08-16-29	3	W.D.C. to Santo Domingo
Sanderson, Lawson H.M.	1st Lt.	04-22-21	12-13-27		08-31-29	4	W.D.C. to Santo Domingo
Bradley, Basil G. (100)	1st Lt.	04-22-21	12-13-27			5	W.D.C. to Santo Domingo
Rucker, Charles W.	G.Sgt.	04-22-21	12-13-27	(1st USMC enlisted)		6	W.D.C. to Santo Domingo
Bourne, Louis M. (097)	Maj.	01-14-28				7	Miami to Managua flight
Wodarczyk, Michael	Ch.MG	02-28-28			09-07-28	8	Nicaragua, troop rescue

NAME	RANK	EVENT	APPR.	CERTIF. ISSUE	MEDAL PRES.	NUMBER OF AWARD MEDAL	EVENT/NOTES
U.S. MARINE CORPS							
Lamson-Scribner, Frank H.	1st Lt.	01-14-28	04-14-30			9	Nicaragua bandit fight
Weir, Frank D.	1st Lt.	01-14-28	04-14-30			10	Nicaragua bandit fight
Munsch, Albert S.	M.T.Sgt.	01-14-28	04-14-30			11	Nicaragua bandit fight
Parker, Alton N.	Capt.	1929/30	10-23-30			12	Antarctic flight
Mitchell, Ralph J.	Maj.	06-19-30				13	Nicaragua, Squad.
Johnson, Byron F.	Capt.	06-19-30				14	Nicaragua bandit fight
Young, John S. E.	1st Lt.	06-19-30			01-23-32	15	Nicaragua bandit fight
Fike, Charles L.	1st Lt.	06-19-30	-30?			16	Nicaragua bandit fight
Hart, John N.	2nd Lt.	06-19-30	03-05-31		01-23-32	17	Nicaragua bandit fight
Page, Arthur H.	Capt	07-21-30				18	Omaha to Anacostia
Becker, Herbert P.	1st Lt.	07-22-31	03-21-32?		(Hoover?)	19	Nicaragua, Coto River
Heritage, Gordon W.	SSgt.	07-22-31	03-21-32			20	Nicaragua, Coto River
Torner, Hilmer N.	Cpl.	03-22-32	05-27-32		06-01-32	21	Emerg. Rescue & Land.
Williams, Neal G.	Sgt./Lt.	07-06-32	03-20-33		05-18-33	22	Nicaragua + WWII
Rutledge, Raymond P.[2]	2nd Lt.	05-23-32	-32?			23	Nicaragua, patrol rescue
Evans, Francis T.	Capt.	02-13-17	02-25-36	(F.D.R.?)	06-10-36	24	Spins & Loops tests
Jerome, Clayton C.	Capt.	04-23-37	08-29-38?		03-24-39?	25	Rescue, Guatamala
U.S. COAST GUARD							
Olson, C. B.	Lt.	06 - 1935			05-12-38	1 (Sec. Morganthau)	Sea Emergency
Leahy, Frank Ashton	Lt./Cdr	05-21-37	11-09-38			2	Sea Emergency

1 Heroism
2 Posthumous
3 These four medal numbers were awarded to personnel; Alexander, McDonough, Reid and Murtha in some sequence.
4 The letter requesting medal engraving for Soucek, Dillon, Burkett, Whitehead and Alexander was dated 10-27-30.

Note: Byrd's expeditions: North Pole, 1926; Atlantic crossing, 1927; Little America 1929; Little America II, 1934.

BIBLIOGRAPHY

BINGHAM, Hiram, "An Explorer in the Air Service", NEW HAVEN, Yale University Press, 1920.

BLAKENEY, Jane, "Heroes, U.S. Marine Corps, 1861 - 1955, Armed Forces Awards - Flags", U.S. Marine Corps, 1957, Guthrie Lithograph Co. Inc.

BOHANNON, Shawn, M., "Biography of Brigadier General Arthur B. McDaniel", Office of History, San Antonio Air Logistics Center, Kelly AFB, Texas, May 1, 1997, and personal communications.

BOYNE, WALTER J., "Silver Wings, a History of the United States Air Force", Simon and Schuster, 1993.

BROWN, Riley, "Men, Wind, and Sea, the Story of the Coast Guard", Blue Ribbon Books.

CROUCH, Tom D., "The Eagle Aloft, Two Centuries of the Balloon in America", Smithsonian Institution, Smithsonian Institution Press, Washington, D.C. 1983.

DAVISON, F. Trubee, Records of the Office, Asst. Sec of War for Air, 1926-47, correspondence in the National Archives, RG 107, 207 et al, including Adm. Byrd, Ira Eaker, Congress and USMC data.

DEPARTMENT OF THE AIR FORCE, Air Force Historical Research Agency, Maxwell AFB, AL, personal communication February 1995, DFC List (1-14, 17, 18, 25, and 26) and copies of WD GOs 1927 through 1938.

DEPARTMENT OF THE ARMY, Administrative Assistant to the Secretary, 105 Army Pentagon, also Total Army Personnel Command, Alexandria, VA., personal communications April 1995 with letters re 1927 securing of designs, and engraving DFC for Charles Lindbergh.

DEPARTMENT OF THE ARMY, The Institute of Heraldry, Fort Belvoir, VA., personal communication March 1995 with data re DFC, copies of Public Law (Acts of Congress), and General Orders/letters of the War Department.

DEPARTMENT OF THE NAVY, Awards and Decorations Branch, Washington Navy Yard, Citation and award data, personal correspondence.

DeVORKIN, David H., AIR AND SPACE magazine, Smithsonian, "The Height of Ambition", April/May 1991 (balloonists).

FRITZ, Russel R., "The Medals of Clyde Pangborn", Journal of the Orders and Medals Society, Volume 41, No. 6, June 1990.

GLEIM, Al, editor, (not listed on publication). "Reprinted Supplements, Decorations, United States Army, - 1862 - 1926 - "(period 1 Jan, 1927 to 30 June, 1941)", Planchet Press PUB 2B. Citations of awards including the Distinguished Flying Cross.

HOOVER, HERBERT, Letter of presentation with award details for Eugene B. Ely, February 13, 1933, copy courtesy National Archives.

HISTORICAL DIVISION, "U.S. Marine Corps, Marine Aviation in the Philippines", 1951.

LEATHERNECK MAGAZINE, July 1933.

MAGUIRE, Jon A., "More Silver Wings, Pinks & Greens", Schiffer Publishing Ltd., 1996.

MARINE CORPS, HQ United States, Historical Museums Division, Biographicqal data and/or citations on 15 USMC pilots and other airmen, personal correspondence.

MILLER, Frances Trevelyan, "The World in the Air, The Story of Flying in Pictures", Volume Two, G.P. PUTNAM S SONS, 1930.

MINGOS, Howard, "American Heroes of the War in the Air", Volume One, Lanciar Publishers Inc. 1943.

NATIONAL ARCHIVES, Personal communication re DFC awards, June through December 1941.

NATIONAL PERSONNEL RECORDS CENTER, Military Personnel Records, St. Louis, MO. Award Cards for War Department awards to 80 persons plus searches for 24 more that could not be located. Twenty U.S. Navy and 20 U.S. Marine Corps personnel award cards or citation letters were received from here and other sources.

NEVIN, DAVID, ET AL, "The Pathfinders", Time Life Books, 1980.

THE NEW YORK TIMES, selected articles, 1927 through 1941.

OFFICE OF NAVAL OPERATIONS/BUREAU OF NAVAL WEAPONS, "United States Naval Aviation 1910-60", 1960, NAVWEPS 00-80P-1.

O'NEIL, Paul and the Editors of Time-Life Books. "Barnstormers & Speed Kings", TIME- LIFE BOOKS, 1981.

RECRUITING NEWS, "Parachute Tester Decorated" (re Sgt. Bottriell, Chapter Five), June 15, 1933.

"1972 REGISTER OF GRADUATES and Former Cadets of the United States Military Academy", Association of Graduates U.S.M.A.

STEVENS, Captain Albert W., "Exploring the Stratosphere", THE NATIONAL GEOGRAPHIC MAGAZINE, October 1934, (Chapter Five).

WOOD AND CANVAS HEROES

Photographic Credits

National Air and Space Museum, Smithsonian Institute, SI negative numbers:
Fig. 1, A-34794-B; Fig. 3, 4A7526; Fig. 10, 7B-3051;
Fig. 11, A-4413-A; Fig. 25, not provided; Fig. 28, A-4146.

Pensacola Naval Air Station:
Fig. 2.

National Archives and Records Administration, P&P Division, negative numbers:
Fig. 4, 4A-42090; Fig. 13, 80-G-458568 (306 NT 28901);
Fig. 14, 208065; Fig. 18, B8790; Fig. 20, 5338AS;
Fig. 21, B11271; Fig. 29, 206799; Fig. 31, PN-10850-1-32;
Fig. 32, B9581; Fig. 34, Photo Lt. J. F. Phillips & MSgt. G. B. Gilbert, B9619; Fig. 35, B11279; Fig. 37, SC-98425;
Fig. 43, B11260.

Missouri Historical Society, St. Louis, Missouri, Lindbergh Collection:
Fig. 6, box 297, #363, photo Pacific and Atlantic;
Fig. 7, box 279, #450, photo Underwood and Underwood;
Fig. 9, Index book box 2.

San Diego Aerospace Museum:
Fig. 16; Fig. 24; Fig. 36.

Library of Congress:
Fig. 19, none, photo Associated Press; Fig. 22, none:
Fig. 33, photo Richard H. Stewart, FSA - Office of War Information Collection, LC-USW34-038172-B;
Fig. 41, none, photo Associated Press; Fig. 42, none;
Fig. 44, none, photo Associated Press.

Wright University Library Collection:
Fig. 23.

Airmen Memorial Museum:
Fig. 26.

"Leatherneck, Magazine of the Marines":
Fig. 39, courtesy editor, Col. W. G. Ford, USMC, retired.

All other photographs are the property of the author or private parties, and may not be used without the express written permission of the author/James W. Patrick Publishing.

INDEX OF NAMES

Name	Page(s)
Acosta, Bert	xvi, 22-24
Adams, Secretary of Navy	68, 80, 82
Akers, Frank L.	128
Alcock, John	xv, 1
Aldworth, Richard T.	124, 125
Alexander, Claude G.	77, 79, 80, 82, 87
Amundsen, Roald	34
Anderson, Charles	89
Anderson, Frederick L.	119, 121
Anderson, Orville A.	101, 103, 105, 120, 121, 148
Andrews, Frank M.	137
Armstrong, Frank A., Jr.	126
Arnold, Henry H. "Hap"	120, 122, 123, 133, 146
Arnold, Henry H., Jr.	123
Arnold, Leslie	45, 63
Balbo, Italo	118, 119
Balchen, Bernt	22-24, 82
Baldwin, Thomas	ix, x
Becker, Herbert P.	109, 110
Bellonte, Maurice	42
Bennett, Floyd	xvi, 24
Benton, John W.	3, 5-7
Berkeley, R. C.	114
Billingsley, William D.	xiii
Boardman, Russell N.	93-95
Boothman, John	71
Bossom, Alfred C.	89
Bottriel, Ralph W.	95-97
Bourne, Louis M.	49
Boushey, Homer A.	136
Bowley, Albert J.	103, 105

Bowlin, William M.	126, 127
Boyden, Hayne D.	27, 29, 30, 50
Bradley, Basil G.	31
Bronte, Emory B.	35, 98-100
Brown, Arthur	xv, 1
Bruner, Donald L.	97
Buckman, Donald W.	124, 125
Burkett, Eugene F.	80, 82, 87
Bushnell, W.	55
Byrd, Richard E.	xvi, 3, 21-24, 33, 55, 72-74, 82, 84, 126
Caldwell, Willliam W.	76
Cavin, Doyle J.	108, 109
Chamberlin, Clarence	2, 23
Chambers, W. I.	xiv
Champion, C. C.	21
Chanute, Octave	ix
Chennault, Claire	55
Christmas, William	x
Cochran, Jacqueline	133
Coli, Frances	2
Connor, Frank B.	123
Coolidge, Calvin	5, 11-13, 17, 23, 24, 38, 63
Cornwell, Delbert S.	25, 26, 49
Costes, Dieudonne	39-43, 51, 72, 93
Cousland, Cornelius W.	99, 100
Craig, Malin	75, 77
Crane, Carl J.	143
Crosby, W. S.	108
Crosson, Joe	117
Crumrine, Clarence E.	44-47
Cuddihy, George T.	68-70
Cunningham, Alfred A.	xii
Curtis, Charles	92
Curtiss, Edward B.	25
Curtiss, Glenn H.	x-xii, xiv, xv, 96, 97
Dargue, Donald	8

Dargue, Herbert A.	3-8
Davis, Dwight F.	6, 15, 56, 58
Davis, William V., Jr.	26, 34, 48, 49
Davison, F. Trubee	7, 48, 58, 73
de Pinedo, Francesco	38, 40, 43
Dillon, Wallace M.	80-82, 87
Dobberpfhul, Erwin J.	148
Doolittle, James	xv, 2, 56, 61, 62, 65-67, 71, 94, 135, 148
Dugan, Richard I.	120
Eaker, Ira C.	3, 5-8, 59-61, 148
Earhart, Amelia - Mrs. Putnam	33, 91-93, 95
Eielson, Carl B.	56, 57
Ellis, Dross	135, 136
Ellyson, Theodore G.	xi, xii, 33
Ely, Eugene B.	xi, 106-109
Ely, Eugene J.	107, 108
Ely, Hanson E.	107, 108
Ely, Nathan D.	106 -108
English, Joseph	45, 47
Ent, Uzal G.	47, 48
Eoff, James H.	150
Eubeck, Eugene L.	148
Evans, Francis T.	xiii, 129-131
Evert, Paul	47
Fairchild, Muir S.	3, 6, 8, 10
Fechet, James E.	74
Fike, Charles L.	85
Fitzmaurice, James C.	24, 38, 39, 43
Fonck, René	2
Forsythe, Albert	89
Foulois, Benjamin	xi, xii, 7, 61,65, 67, 90, 96
Gatty, Harold	94, 95
Gavin, Arthur	33
Giles, Barney M.	123
Gilmore, Earl	71
Gives, John L.	120

Goebel, Arthur C.	34-36, 48, 49
Gray, Hawthorne C.	17-20, 34, 36, 47, 101
Greene, Carl F.	141-143
Griffith, John S.	122
Guymon, V. M.	87
Halverson, Harry	60, 61
Hamilton, Donald E.	123
Hamilton, George	45
Harding, John	63
Harris, Samuel R.	144, 147
Hart, John N.	84-86
Hatfield, Vernon O.	149
Haynes, Caleb V.	138-141, 148
Hegenberger, Albert	16, 17, 22, 35, 98-100, 148
Heritage, Gordon W.	110, 111
Herrick, Ambassador	40
Hine, Virgil	143
Hinton, Walter	1, 2, 106
Hoffer, Orlo S.	111
Holloman, George V.	143
Hook, Ray W.	60, 61
Hoover, Herbert	42, 68, 92, 93, 106, 107, 110
Hudnell, William T.	146, 147
Hughes, Howard	33, 133
Humphries, Fred E.	xi
Hurley, Patrick J.	74, 107
Irvin, Frank G.	122
Jerome, Clayton C.	153, 154
Johnson, Alfred H.	141-143
Johnson, Byron F.	85
Jones, Ulysses G.	75
Jones, Ulysses G., Jr.	76
June, Harold I. J.	24, 82, 83, 92
Kelly, Oakley G.	10, 34-36
Kelsey, Benjamin S.	66, 135, 136
Kenney, George C.	10, 47

Kepner, William E.	101, 103, 105
Kirkpatrick, Ross	44, 45, 47
Koehl, Herman	24, 38, 39, 43
LaGuardia, Fiorello	125
Lahm, Frank P.	x, xi
Lamson-Scribner, Frank H.	51, 52
Langley, Samuel	ix, x
Lansdowne, Zachary	152
Lassiter, William	75
Lazarus, Willard W.	145, 147
Leahy, Frank A.	155
LeBrix, Joseph	39, 42, 43
Lee, General	114, 115
Lindbergh, Charles L.	xvi, 2, 3, 7, 10-16, 56, 92
Long, James D.	45, 47
Lowe, T. S. C.	ix
Lowrey, William W.	151
Luke, Frank	xvi
MacArthur, Douglas	10
MacReady, John A.	10, 34-36
Maitland, Lester	15-17, 22, 35, 99
Malmgren, Finn	34
Martin, Frederic	63
Maughan, Russell	2, 34, 36, 37
Maxson, Lisle	33
McCants, John R.	151
McClellan, Hez	121
McCoy, Frank	124
McDaniel, Arthur B.	3, 6, 8, 9
McDonnell, John B.	147
McDonough, Andrew	80, 82, 87
McDuff, Francis H.	119, 121
McGinnis, Knefler	128, 129
McKay, Donald B.	149
McKinley, Ashley C.	24, 72-74, 82
Mendez, Benjamin	61, 62

Meredith, Russell L.	98-100
Meyer, Walter T.	75
Mitchell, Billy	7, 36
Mitchell, Ralph J.	84, 85
Moor, Robert D.	90, 91
Morgan, Stanley R.	117
Munsch, Albert S.	51
Murtha, William J.	80, 82, 87
Mussolini, Benito	39, 118
Neely, Harold L.	144, 147
Neff, Frank D.	91
Nelson, Eric H.	xv, 44, 45, 47, 63
Nobile, Umberto	34
Northcliffe, Lord Alfred	1, 2
Noville, George	3, 22, 23
Nungessor, Charles	2
Nutt, Clifford C.	44, 45, 47, 96
O'Donnell, Emmett "Rosie", Jr.	148
Olds, Robert	137, 138
Olson, C. B.	154, 155
O'Malley, Thomas F.	145-147
Orteig, Raymond	2
Osipoff, Walter S.	150, 151
Page, Arthur H.	87
Pangburn, Clyde	71
Parker, Alton N.	83, 84
Patrick, James H., Jr.	123
Patrick, Mason	xi, 4, 7
Paunack, Robert R.	xiii, 26, 27, 30
Pellegrini, Aldo	118
Pelter, Joseph A.	126, 127
Perce, Earle B.	150
Pershing, John	126
Phelps, Otto R.	149
Polando, John N.	93-95
Post, Wiley	94, 95, 117, 133

Name	Pages
Price, George E.	145, 147
Pride, A. M.	33
Provost, Maurice	71
Putnam, Mrs. - see Earhart	
Quesada, Elwood R.	60, 61
Ramscheusen, Roger	33
Rawlings, Edwin W.	75
Rawson, Kennett L.	89
Read, Albert C.	xiii, 1, 2, 134
Reeves, J. M.	77
Reid, Thomas G.	80, 82, 87
Richardson, Holden G.	2
Richter, John P.	62, 63, 65, 67, 143
Rickenbacker, Eddie V.	xvi, 72
Ride, Sally	92
Robbins, Augustine W.	135
Robinson, Charles McK.	3, 6, 10
Rodgers, John	xii
Rogers, Will	95, 117
Roosevelt, Franklin D.	66, 124, 128, 131, 151
Rosendahl, Charles E.	152
Roth, Benjamin	73, 74
Rowell, Ross E.	27-30, 50, 51, 114
Rucker, Charles W.	31
Rutledge, Raymond P.	113, 114
Sanderson, Lawson H. M.	31, 114, 115
Saufley, Richard C.	xiv
Schilt, C. F.	xvi, 33
Schmidt, Hugh	33
Schofield, Harold W.	xiii
Scott, Russell	124
Seifert, Frank W.	143
Selfridge, Thomas E.	x
Senn, Thomas	99
Settle, T. G. W.	55
Shoemaker, J. M.	83

Sikorsky, Igor	2
Smith, Dean C.	73, 74
Smith, Ernest L.	62, 99
Smith, Lowell	xv, 2, 35, 45, 62-65, 143
Snow, Ashley C.	150
Soucek, Apollo	77-80, 87
Soucek, Zeus	33, 77
Spaatz, Carl "Tooey"	8, 59-61
Standley, William H.	128, 129
Stevens, Albert W.	1, 101, 103-106, 120, 121, 148
Stone, David L.	141, 142
Stone, Elmer F.	xiv
Street, St. Clair	44, 47
Street, St. Clair, Jr.	47
Summers, Robert F.	75
Sutton, Harry A.	67
Sweet, George C.	xi
Thaden, Louise	133
Thompson, Bernard S.	3, 6
Tomlinson, W. G.	55
Torner, Hilmer	111, 112
Towers, John H.	xii, xiii, 134
Turner, Roscoe	71, 133
Turner, Thomas C.	30, 31
von Huenefeld, E. Gunther	24, 38, 39, 43
von Zeppelin, Ferdinand	ix
Wallace, James H.	126
Watts, W. C.	127
Weddington, Leonard D.	3, 6
Wedell, James	133
Weir, Frank B.	51, 52
Westover, Oscar	133
Whitehead, Ennis C.	3, 6, 10, 47
Whitehead, Richard F.	80, 82, 87
Whitney, Raymond U.	145, 147
Wilbur, Curtis D.	21, 23

Wilkins, Sir Hubert	56
Williams, Alford	56, 67-70
Williams, Neal	112-115
Winens, Edwin B.	45
Wodarczyk, Michael	28, 29, 50, 51
Wolfe, Franklin C.	141, 142
Woodring, Harry H.	122, 139
Woodring, Irvin A.	76
Woolsey, Clinton F.	3, 5-7
Wright Brothers	x, 57, 59
Wright, Orville	x, xv, 57, 58
Wright, Wilbur	x, 57, 58
Wurtsmith, Paul B.	47
Wyatt, Ben H.	25, 26, 78, 82
Young, John S. E.	85, 86

ABOUT THE AUTHOR

James W. Patrick retired after 36 years with North American Rockwell Space Systems Division. During his tenure he served as Technical Writer - Manager of Technical Publications. He directed preparation of Flight Crew Operations Procedures and In-Flight Checklist for Apollo Astronauts. In advanced engineering, he authored several research and study reports including a Crew Operations Definition for an advanced Manned Space Station, as well as numerous reports on advanced space vehicles.

Mr. Patrick is a collector of military orders and medals, and a member of the Orders and Medals Society of America and the Orders and Medals Research Society of Great Britain.

The author wishes to recognize the *Orders and Medals Society of America (OMSA)* which promotes the retention of medals and records about them, enhances their recognition, and researches and publishes the stories about the men and women who won them. This is also true for the *Orders and Medals Research Society (OMRS)* of Great Britain.